THE
Archive Photographs
SERIES

HENDON TO
FARNBOROUGH
SBAC DISPLAYS 1932-1972

The sixteen all-black Hawker Hunters of 111 Squadron, the famous *Black Arrows*, which set standards for aerobatic teams between 1957 and 1961. In this 1959 photo they are led by a two-seater Hunter T.7.

THE
Archive Photographs
SERIES

HENDON TO FARNBOROUGH
SBAC DISPLAYS 1932-1972

Compiled by
Mike Hooks

CHALFORD

First published 1996
Copyright © Mike Hooks, 1996

The Chalford Publishing Company
St Mary's Mill, Chalford,
Stroud, Gloucestershire, GL6 8NX

ISBN 0 7524 0372 9

Typesetting and origination by
The Chalford Publishing Company
Printed in Great Britain by
Redwood Books, Trowbridge

Front Cover Illustration
The second SBAC Display – Hendon, 1933, with a surprisingly small number of
visitors in the static park. In the foreground, the Percival Gull G-ACHA
experimentally fitted with a Napier Javelin engine; behind, an early
D.H. Tiger Moth, G-ACFA and D.H. Dragon G-ACCE with its wings folded.

A typical Farnborough show scene; this was in 1959 and in the foreground are Hunter XG135, Saunders-Roe P.531 G-APVM and Jet Provost CJ701 of the Ceylon Air Force. In the centre are Gnats XN326 (a single-seater) and XM691 with a profusion of helicopters in the background.

Contents

Explanations

This is a book about aircraft which have appeared at the SBAC shows although it has only been possible to include a selection of the many types exhibited. It has not always been possible to show aircraft at the event being covered, nevertheless the actual individual aircraft are illustrated. Ground shots only would have been very boring so I have attempted to provide a good mix. My apologies to anyone whose favourite type does not appear!

Changes throughout the years in ownership of companies present some apparent anomalies, for instance Armstrong Siddeley later became Bristol Siddeley, Bristol's engine Division became part of Rolls-Royce and so on.

Putting together a picture book inevitably leaves the author with doubts on the origins of some of the illustrations, so I take this opportunity to thank those unnamed photographers whose work is not acknowledged. My thanks also to Richard Riding of *Aeroplane Monthly* for permission to reproduce pictures from their archives, to fellow author Derek James, to Duncan Simpson, former Deputy Director, SBAC and Hawker test pilot, and to the SBAC for allowing access to their archives.

Abbreviations can become tiresome so have been used sparingly, as follows:

> AACU – Anti-Aircraft Cooperation Unit
> A&AEE – Aircraft & Armament Experimental Establishment
> AFEE – Airborne Forces Experimental Establishment
> AOP – Air Observation Post
> ehp – equivalent horsepower
> MAEE – Maritime Aircraft Experimental Establishment
> RAAF – Royal Australian Air Force
> RAE – Royal Aircraft Establishment
> RRE – Royal Radar Establishment
> SCBS – Strike Command Bombing School
> shp – shaft horsepower
> SOC – Struck off charge
> Spec – Specification

Finally, B Conditions markings are temporary identification used by manufacturers during test flying, while Impressed denotes commandeered for military use during the Second World War.

Introduction

Visitors to the biennial Exhibition and Flying Display of the Society of British Aerospace Companies at Farnborough can see the latest aircraft from many countries in a concentrated two-and-a-half hour flying display, perhaps the most controlled and carefully timed display anywhere in the world.

The variety of aircraft on show ranges from small private touring types to the largest airliners and includes helicopters, trainers, fighters, bombers, reconnaissance aircraft and experimental types, although it has to be said that these days there are few of the last named.

It was not always so, neither has the Show always been an international event or in the style presented today, so how has it evolved over the years?

The Society of British Aircraft Constructors, its original title, was formed in 1916 at the height of the First World War and entered the exhibition arena in 1920 when it cooperated with the Society of Motor Manufacturers and Traders to mount a show at Olympia and twenty-eight aircraft were present, of which twenty-three were British.

The SBAC continued to support the Olympia shows until 1929; meanwhile the Air Ministry staged the first of many displays at Hendon to show the British public how the Royal Air Force was progressing and these ran annually until June 1937 when Hendon had become, it was felt, too small for the increasing size and airfield requirements of military aircraft.

One of the features of the RAF Displays was an enclosure for prototypes, the New Types Park, and in 1932 the SBAC prevailed upon the Air Ministry to retain this until the day following the RAF Display so that the Society could include further aircraft from its member companies and invite foreign guests to view the latest products of the British aircraft industry, both on the ground and in the air.

So was born the first SBAC Display, held on 27 June 1932, when a total of thirty-four aircraft were shown. There was no public admission, nor was photography permitted but after strong reaction from the press, cameras were allowed from the 1933 event. Fortunately, there are ample pictures available of the types shown in 1932, even if they were not taken at the show.

From that beginning grew the remainder of the pre-war events which continued until 1937. However, the last event to be held at Hendon took place on 1 July 1935; the work involved in clearing up after public attendance at the RAF Displays prior to the SBAC's private show was becoming too arduous and the Society had reached the same conclusion about Hendon as the Air Ministry, although two years earlier!

Consideration was given to transferring the show to Olympia but it was obvious that the flying display was an essential part of the event so the new venue chosen was Hatfield, home of the de Havilland aircraft company and its technical school, the London Aerospace Club and an RAF Reserve Training School.

As it turned out, only two shows were held at Hatfield, in 1936-37; in 1937 foreigners were banned because of the worsening international situation but the show was spread over two days. It was planned to admit the public on the second day from the following year, 1938, but in fact 1937 was the last of the pre-war shows and it was to be another eleven years before public admittance was to become a regular feature.

The first post-war show was held at Radlett, near St Albans, then the Handley Page airfield on 12-13 September 1946, when Britain's aircraft manufacturers were able to present the products of the company's largest industry, showing jet aircraft for the first time.

The next show, in 1947 was also held at Radlett, but already thought was being given to finding a suitable venue where the public could be admitted. Whether this was through consideration for the public or realisation that admittance charges would help to finance the

The second SBAC display was held at Hendon in 1933 and was the first at which cameras were allowed. At this end of the static park are the Napier Javelin-engined Percival Gull G-ACHA, D.H. Fox Moth G-ABXS, Spartan Cruiser II G-ACDX and the sole Spartan Clipper G-ACEG.

show is not clear! It is true, however, that these charges have always been a very important factor in the financing of the show, the prime purpose of which is to boost trade, therefore costs to the exhibitors should be kept as low as possible. It follows that substantial income from public admission helps to lower these costs.

A feature of these early shows was a 'circus' of aircraft in which a small group would take off and fly past in succession. In later years when flying regulations became more strict, the aircraft displays, apart from aerobatic teams, were usually single or at the most, double items.

In 1948 the show moved to its present location at Farnborough where the layout provided a natural amphitheatre for viewing the flying display and the public were admitted for the final weekend. Held from 7-12 September, it marked a large increase in the number of trade and technicians days and the show continued to expand, finally reaching eight days, with the last three open to the public. In more recent times, at the request of exhibitors for whom costs are vitally important, the show has been cut by one day with public admission reverting to only the final weekend.

The period covered by this book, 1932 to 1972, was chosen largely to illustrate the multitude of British aircraft types which appeared between those years. From 1966, foreign aircraft could be shown in the flying display if they used a British engine or major British components, but they had to be sponsored by British partners. From 1972 it became Farnborough Europe, with

Hendon 1933 and the Handley Page H.P.47 K2773 flew past the prototype Avro Anson K4771, Cierva C.30A G-ACWO, the only British Bullpup J9051, the prototype Supermarine Seagull A2-1 for Australia (later known in the RAF as the Walrus) and the prototype Bristol Bombay K3585 – the only one built by that company as the fifty production aircraft were built by Short.

entries accepted from European manufacturers, but in 1974 the show became fully international.

Until 1962 the show had been held annually, apart of course from the wartime period, but it then became biennial, in even years. Aircraft development was taking longer and the move to biennial slotted in nicely with the Paris Air Show held in odd years. In 1964, the SBAC changed its name, but not initials, to the Society of British Aerospace Companies, reflecting the expansion of interest in the industry.

Many of the aircraft shown post-war turned up year after year as best selling types in different variants – examples are the de Havilland Dove, Hawker Hunter and English Electric Lightning to name a few. The 1950s and '60s were notable for the number of prototypes and test-bed aircraft shown, many of the latter testing new jet and turboprop engines for the next generation of military aircraft and civil airliners.

Although there were some private venture prototypes, a number were the result of specifications issued to the industry and several companies competed for orders. Examples included the Avro Athena and Boulton Paul Balliol trainers, both originally to have turboprop engines, of which the Balliol won the contract but with a Rolls-Royce Merlin as standard, and the Percival Provost and Handley Page H.P.R.2 trainers, winner of which was the Provost.

Many of the 1950s and, '60s shows enjoyed considerable Service support – in 1958 no fewer than 143 RAF and RN aircraft took part including fly-pasts by forty-five Hawker Hunters and forty-five Gloster Javelins. Service participation was always very popular with the public, in

Part of the New Types Park at Hatfield in 1937 with a selection of prototypes – Airspeed Oxford L4534, Fairey P.4/34 K7555, later developed into the Fulmar, Hawker Henley K5115, Gloster F.5/34 K5604, the unregistered Miles Kestrel with New Types Park number 2, later developed as the Master and the de Havilland Albatross with B Conditions marks E-2.

particular massed assaults on the airfield which included airborne landings, dummy attacks and lots of smoke and noise. Unfortunately, these days Service support is very limited thanks to defence cuts although the point has to be made that it is now extremely difficult for the SBAC to fit in all exhibitors' aircraft requesting slots in the flying programme if it is be kept to a reasonable length.

Finally, although not illustrated, we must not forget the many equipment manufacturers who play a vital role in aerospace. Aircraft are the glamour side of the business, but they could not exist without the myriad number of items supplied by the equipment industry.

This is a book about aircraft and as such seeks to show some of the more interesting types; Some made it while others did not for various reasons but the 'might have beens' are nevertheless interesting. Also included are just a few of the personalities who have visited the shows or have taken part in them.

The decision to stop at 1972 was taken as it is a logical point before the show became fully international, since it aims primarily to illustrate British achievement in an industry which has produced some remarkable aircraft such as the world's first jet and turboprop airliners, the D.H. Comet and Vickers Viscount, and the world's first vertical take off fighter, the Hawker (now BAe) Harrier. Development nowadays is so costly that many new designs are joint efforts between international partners and we shall never again experience the heyday of all-British aircraft with all-British engines (remember the de Havilland and Bristol companies?) so let us look back with nostalgia and affection at our past triumphs (and failures, it must be said) and recall our debt to those designers, manufacturers and pilots of a bygone era.

Radlett and the Handley Page airfield in 1947. The third de Havilland D.H.108 VW120 attracts interest, while beyond are the Ghost-engined de Havilland Vampire F.1 TG443, Reid & Sigrist Desford G-AGOS, Hawker Sea Fury FB.X TF955 and Blackburn S.28/43 RT651. Also visible are Fairey Firefly FR.IV TW695, Firefly Trainer MB750, Gloster Meteor F.4 RA449, Heston A.2/45 VL529, Westland Wyvern TF.I TS371 and Auster AOP.VI 16658 in Canadian Army colours.

The move to Farnborough, 1948. This shows most of the static park and is a nice recognition test for the enthusiast! The old hangars have long since gone and that area is now covered by exhibition halls every two years. Remarkably few people seem to be among the aircraft.

Farnborough, 1952. The hospitality chalets were minimal structures but the President's tent was more palatial! Larger aircraft on show included Canadian Pacific's de Havilland Comet IA CF-CUM, prototypes of the Bristol Britannia, G-ALBO, and Short Sperrin VX158 and Avro Shackleton MR.2 WG531. The monster at left foreground is the prototype Blackburn & General Aircraft Universal Freighter WF320 which went into production for the RAF as the Beverley.

Blackburn Beverley C.1 XB289, the eighteenth production aircraft of forty-seven built for the RAF, emplanes troops on the Farnborough runway in 1956 prior to its demonstration. Beverleys served from March 1956 until a final fly-past in December 1968. Powered by four 2,850 hp Bristol Centaurus engines, they were, on introduction, the RAF's largest aircraft.

One
The Thirties
1932-1937

The early years of this period were dominated by the biplane, certainly in the military field, and it was only by 1935 that the monoplane began to take over. The figures were as follows, with biplanes first and monoplanes in brackets for each of the shows: 1932- 23 (11); 1933- 33 (12); 1934- 26 (12); 1935- 17 (19); 1936- 11 (25); 1937- 7 (30). Additionally, in each of the last three years there was one rotary-wing craft.

At the time of the first show in 1932, the Royal Air Force's front line aircraft consisted solely of biplanes. Fighter Command had nine squadrons of Bristol Bulldogs while Bomber Command's most modern type was the Boulton & Paul Sidestrand.

New civil aircraft shown in 1932 which made their mark in service included the Handley Page H.P.42 biplane and Armstrong Whitworth monoplane airliners, both ordered by Imperial Airways, while the de Havilland company showed the Puss Moth monoplane plus Tiger Moth and Fox Moth biplanes.

By 1937, the last show before the Second World War, the RAF's expansion programme was beginning to show fruit; both Spitfire and Hurricane had flown, together with three bombers which were to see service in numbers, the Armstrong Whitworth Whitley, Bristol Blenheim and Handley Page Hampden. The Fairey Swordfish, already almost obsolete, earned an enviable reputation throughout the war, outlasting its replacement, the Fairey Albacore. Other types which enjoyed a long and successful career, even in unspectacular roles were the Avro Anson, Supermarine Walrus and Westland Lysander.

As photography was not permitted at the 1932 show, some of the actual aircraft participating are shown at other locations. This is the Saro Cloud amphibian K2681, wearing New Types Park No 12, used in the 1931 RAF Display. Employed on experimental work, it was eventually SOC on 28 April 1938.

J9130 was the prototype Handley Page H.P.38, later named Heyford. Powered by two 575 hp Rolls-Royce Kestrel engines, it was used for trials by various squadrons but was destroyed when it crashed at North Coates Fittes on 8 July 1932, a mere eleven days after the SBAC show. Production Heyfords served with eleven squadrons between 1934 and 1939, 124 being delivered to the RAF.

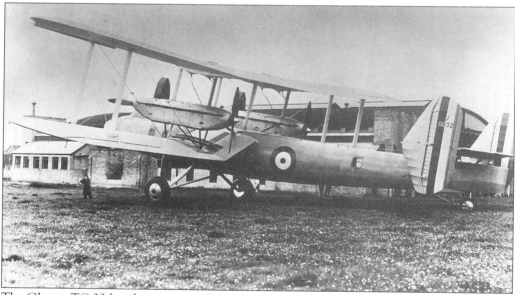

The Gloster TC.33 bomber transport J9832 had four 580 hp Rolls-Royce Kestrel steam-cooled engines mounted back-to-back in pairs and was the company's only four-engined aircraft. It flew on 23 February 1932 and appeared at the RAF and SBAC events in June. Various shortcomings precluded orders and it was last recorded as being with Flight Refuelling Ltd before being SOC on 30 May 1940.

Armstrong Whitworth's A.W.XV Atalanta set new standards of streamlining for British airliners when it appeared at the 1932 show. Powered by four 340 hp Armstrong Siddeley Serval engines, it could carry up to seventeen passengers. Eight were bought by Imperial Airways; G-ABPI was sold to India as VT-AEF in August 1933 and later served as DG453 with the Indian Air Force until SOC in June 1944.

G-ABEG, shown in 1932, was the seventh Westland Wessex airliner. With three 140 hp Armstrong Siddeley Genet Major engines, it was used as a demonstrator until acquired by Imperial Airways in 1933. It was destroyed in a forced landing in 1936 at Chirindu, Northern Rhodesia while serving with Rhodesia and Nyasaland Airways.

Another 1933 view of the line-up on page 8. Additions here are the de Havilland Tiger Moth G-ACFA and Dragon G-ACCE, and one of Air Service Training's Saro Cutty Sarks, either G-ACDP or 'R.

The 1933 park with Westland Wessex G-ACHI making a low pass. In the foreground of the New Types Park wearing No 5 is the Armstrong Whitworth A.W. XVI G-ACCD, subsequently named Scimitar and re-designated A.W.35. It had a 500 hp Armstrong Siddeley Panther engine. One other British aircraft was built but the only customer was the Norwegian Army Air Service who ordered four. G-ACCD was scrapped in 1936.

The massive Blackburn M.1/30A torpedo bomber had an 825 hp Rolls-Royce Buzzard engine and spanned almost fifty feet. Shown here in 1933 before application of its serial K3591, it was technically excellent but did not meet specification requirements and was eventually used by the MAEE, Felixstowe for ditching trials, being SOC in April 1935.

Built to the same specification as the Blackburn design above, the Vickers M.1/30 torpedo bomber S1641 was powered by the same Rolls-Royce Buzzard engine. It appeared at the 1933 show with New Types No 6, not yet applied here. In spite of the massive bridge-like struts it broke up in the air on 23 November 1933, but the crew fortunately escaped.

Another 1933 newcomer was the Gloster SS.19B J9125, prototype of the Gauntlet of which 228 were delivered to the RAF between 1935 and 1937 when they were the fastest fighters in service. They equipped twenty-three units at home and overseas. J9125 was last flown at the RAE on 8 February 1940 and was SOC on 20 January 1941.

The Airspeed Envoy prototype G-ACMT appeared in 1934; developed from the single-engined Courier which was the first British production aircraft to have a retractable undercarriage, it had 185 hp Wolseley A.R.9 engines. Production models had either 200 hp Armstrong Siddeley Lynx or 350 hp Cheetah while export models had other engines. Some fifty Envoys were built, including one for The King's Flight and the type was developed into the Oxford trainer. Several Envoys were used in the Spanish Civil War and G-ACMT, with the wings of G-AEBV, was the aircraft in which the Nationalist General Mola was killed in a crash on 3 June 1937.

The Fairey G.4/31, shown in 1934, was a general-purpose aircraft designed to replace the Fairey Gordon and Westland Wapiti. This is the cleaned-up version with a 750 hp Armstrong Siddeley Tiger engine and B Conditions markings F-1 and New Types No 12. It eventually became K3905 and finished its life at the RAE, its final fate is not known.

Appearing in 1935 was the first Bristol Bulldog IVA, K4292, bought by the Air Ministry to test cowlings for the 640 hp Bristol Mercury engine. There were no British orders for this variant but Finland bought seventeen. K4292 was flown by the makers and A&AEE until becoming instructional airframe 1180M in November 1938.

Among 1935's new types were two Vickers to Spec G.4/31 – a monoplane and a biplane. The latter, Vickers type 253 serialled K2771 and with New Types No 6, featured an early type of geodetic construction and a 635 hp Bristol Pegasus engine. It closely resembled a Parnall design to the same spec and was used by the Bristol Aeroplane Company as an engine test bed until the Second World War when it became instructional airframe 2574M.

The Vickers monoplane (see caption) was the private venture type 287 with B Conditions markings PVO-9. With a 925 hp Bristol Pegasus engine it was obviously superior to the biplane and was developed into the Wellesley of which 176 were built, serving with ten squadrons at home and overseas. Following a crash, PVO-9 was rebuilt as the prototype Wellesley and became K7556, eventually being relegated to instructional use as 1852M in March 1940.

Winner of the speed prize in the 1934 England-Australia race flown by C.W.A. Scott and Tom
Campbell Black, the de Havilland Comet G-ACSS went to Martlesham for RAF trials in 1935
as K5084 and appeared as such at the 1935 show. Damaged and disposed of as scrap, it was
subsequently restored as G-ACSS. Rebuilt to flying condition in the eighties, it belongs to the
Shuttleworth Collection at Old Warden but is no longer flown.

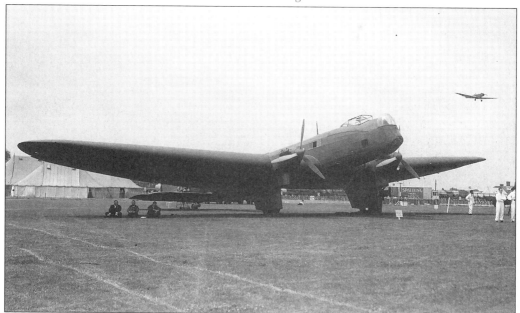

A new bomber was the Fairey Hendon, the prototype of which had been shown in 1934. K1695
was also seen in 1935, but only fourteen were ordered for the RAF, entering service with No 38
Squadron at Mildenhall. Later, one flight was detached to form No 115 Squadron. K1695 was
SOC on 9 September 1938.

Taxying to take off in 1935, only five days after its first flight, is Supermarine Seagull V A2-1 for the Royal Australian Air Force – its display included a loop! Powered by a 775 hp Bristol Pegasus engine, the type was christened Walrus by the RAF and 746 were built, serving with distinction in all theatres in roles from air-sea rescue to dive bombing. RAAF Seagulls served with Nos 9 and 11 Squadrons.

Hawker's private venture P.V.3 fighter with B Conditions marks I-PV3 made its debut in 1935. Its 695 hp Rolls-Royce Goshawk steam-cooled engine was found to be too heavy and the Gloster Gladiator was ordered.

Another 1935 Hawker private venture was the PV-4, marked IPV-4, to Spec G.4/31 as a general-purpose aircraft. Based on the Hart, it had an 800 hp Bristol Pegasus engine originally, but by show time this had been replaced by an 820 hp Pegasus. No orders were forthcoming and, serialled K6926, it was used by Bristol as an engine test-bed until SOC on 29 March 1939.

Yet another contender to Spec G.4/31 was the tadpole-like Handley Page H.P.47 K2773, first flown at Radlett in November 1933. By the time of its show appearance in 1935 it had been fitted with a 750 hp Bristol Pegasus engine, but it was unsuccessful in the competition which had been won by Vickers and was used mainly for engine development before being scrapped in May 1937.

The RAF's last biplane fighter was the Gloster Gladiator; the prototype, to Spec F.7/30 was K5200, shown in 1935. It was a development of the Gauntlet with an 840 hp Bristol Mercury engine and entered RAF service from 1937. Ninety-eight Sea Gladiators were delivered to the Royal Navy, while the type was also supplied to thirteen overseas customers. Total production amounted to 747. K5200 is last recorded with No 2 AACU and was SOC on 12 November 1942.

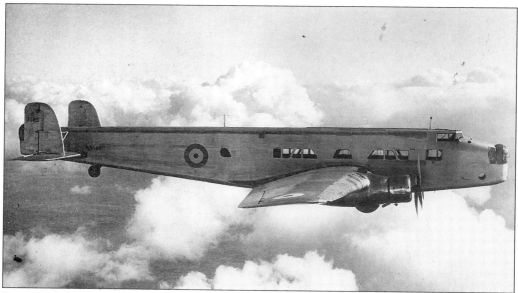

Largest of the 1935 aircraft was the Armstrong Whitworth A.W.23 bomber transport K3585 with 810 hp Armstrong Siddeley Tiger engines. Designed to Spec C.26/31, won by the Bristol Bombay, it was the company's first aircraft to have a retractable undercarriage and formed the design basis for the Whitley bomber. Later used for trials with Flight Refuelling Ltd, it was destroyed at their Ford Aerodrome base in an air raid on 18 August 1940.

Weirdest exhibit in 1935 was the Westland Pterodactyl V K2770, a two-seat fighter to Spec F.3/32 with a 615 hp Rolls-Royce Goshawk steam-cooled engine. The tail-less configuration was chosen to provide an excellent field of fire for the gunner. Certain control difficulties resulted in the design being abandoned and K2770 was dismantled and taken to Farnborough for storage. It was broken up in 1937.

The second production de Havilland Hornet Moth G-ADIS graced the 1935 show, sporting the original pointed wings; most of the 164 production aircraft had the later square-cut wings. Powered by a 130 hp D.H. Gipsy Major engine, it was a popular two-seat cabin aircraft. G-ADIS was impressed on 29 February 1940 as W9391 but did not survive the war, being SOC on 9 June 1944.

The move to Hatfield from Hendon, 1936. This line-up shows the prototype Fairey Battle K4303, one of the first production batch of Fairey Swordfish, K5970 and the prototype Handley Page H.P.52 K4240 which, in production form, became the Hampden. The Battle was looped; it eventually became instructional airframe 1475M and the H.P.52 1490M. The Swordfish went to sea with No 823 Squadron but while attempting to land on HMS *Glorious* on 13 September 1938, overshot arrester wires and fell overboard.

Flown on 17 March 1936, K4586 was the first of two Armstrong Whitworth Whitley prototypes and wore New Types No 9. Powered by 795 hp Armstrong Siddeley Tiger engines, Whitleys were an important part of the RAF's bombing programme in the early war years – later marks had Rolls-Royce Merlins. K4586 finished its life as instructional airframe 4070M.

The 1936 New Types Park. In the foreground, left to right are prototypes of the Hawker Hurricane K5083, Supermarine Spitfire K5054 and the private venture Vickers Venom PVO-10. Careers of the first two need no explanation here; the Venom was a re-designed Jockey with a 625 hp sleeve-valve Bristol Aquila engine. In spite of its superiority in some respects it was not ordered.

The elegant de Havilland Dragonfly G-AEBU, a luxury five-seat tourer powered by 130 hp D.H. Gipsy Major engines flew in February 1936 and was shown at Hatfield that year. It was the first of sixty-six production aircraft and was sold to France as F-AQEU in May 1938.

The public enclosure in 1936. At left, the prototype Westland Lysander K6127, lined up at the centre are GAL Monospars G-AEGX and 'EDY, Blackburn Shark K4882 and the Spitfire prototype K5054. At right, the de Havilland group, D.H.86 E-2, Dragon Rapide YR-DRI and Dragonfly G-AEBU. Flying is the Heston Phoenix G-AEHJ.

A 1936 exhibit was the B.A. Double Eagle six-seater. G-ADVV, the first of two built, was powered by 130 hp D.H. Gipsy Major engines and took part, along with the second, in the 1936 King's Cup and 1938 Isle of Man races. Both were impressed in the Second World War, 'VV becoming ES949 in July 1941. It was SOC in April 1944.

The General Aircraft Monospar ST-25 G-AEDY was shown in 1936 with a single fin and rudder but in the autumn of that year was rebuilt with twin fins and rudders as seen here. More than 100 Monospars were built in several variants but the ST-25, with 95 hp Pobjoy Niagara engines, was the most prolific. G-AEDY crashed at Hanworth, its birthplace, on 10 January 1940, thereby escaping impressment.

This 1936 line-up shows Short Scion G-AEIL, Scion Senior G-AECU, Handley Page H.P.52 K4240, Fairey Swordfish K5970 and Battle K4303. At right are Bristol 142 K7557, 143 R-14 and Bombay K3583.

The silver Westland Lysander prototype K6127 alongside Armstrong Whitworth prototype K4586. Production models of both types were to acquit themselves well in the coming war, but this was in the uneasy peace of 1936. K6127 was with No 1 School of Army Cooperation until being SOC on 23 May 1941.

The Bristol 142 R7557 *Britain First*, built to the order of *Daily Mail* proprietor Lord Rothermere as a high-speed transport for two crew and six passengers, appeared with the Bristol 143 in 1936. Powered by 650 hp Bristol Mercury engines, it had a top speed of 307 mph – 50 mph faster than the RAF's standard fighter, the Gladiator. Lord Rothermere presented the aircraft to the Air Ministry for evaluation as a potential bomber and it evolved into the Blenheim. *Britain First* flew until 1942 when it became instructional airframe 2211M; it was scrapped by Morris Motors at Cowley in 1944.

The Heston Phoenix made a second SBAC appearance at the 1937 show, but this time it was the prototype, G-ADAD. A wooden four-seater with a 200 hp D.H. Gipsy Six engine, it featured a Dowty retractable undercarriage, a revolutionary feature for a high-wing monoplane. Only six were built; the green and silver G-ADAD was allegedly sold to an Athens-based air taxi firm in September 1936 as SX-AAH, which makes its appearance as G-ADAD at the 1937 show unusual!

Designed to the same Spec F.5/34 as the Hurricane and Spitfire, the unnamed Gloster fighter was powered by an 840 hp Bristol Mercury engine but orders were not forthcoming and only two prototypes were built. The first, K5604, appeared at the 1937 show and impressed with its sparkling performance. It faded into obscurity from February 1940 becoming instructional airframe 2232M.

Short C Class Empire flying boat G-AETW *Calpurnia* livened up the lunch period at the 1937 show. Sadly, it crashed in Lake Habbaniyah during a sandstorm on 27 November 1938 killing the pilot, co-pilot and two passengers. In the background are Fairey P.4/34 K7555, a Swordfish, Tipsy S-2 G-AEYG, Heston Phoenix G-ADAD, an Armstrong Whitworth Whitley, Blackburn Shark K8495 and the Gloster F.5/34 K5604.

The little Hafner AR III Gyroplane G-ADMV was a one-off single-seat vertical lift autogyro designed by Raoul Hafner and built by the AR III Construction Co. in Martin-Baker's Denham factory. Powered by a 90 hp Pobjoy Niagara engine, it was tested at Farnborough and then leased to the RAE. Scrapped during the war, it closed the 1937 show and thus has a historical significance. In this view, taken elsewhere, it has attracted the interest of a small boy!

The most streamlined airliner of its day, the de Havilland Albatross appeared at the 1937 show in B Conditions marks E.2. Built of wood, it had four neatly cowled 525 hp D.H. Gipsy Queen engines; the tail design was soon changed to 'endplate' fins. Seven were built for Imperial Airways, E.2 became G-AEVV and with 'EVW was impressed, becoming AX903 and '904. Both were destroyed in crashes at Reykjavik, on 11 August 1941, and 7 April 1942.

A distant view of the 1937 static park at Hatfield. The two D.H.84 Dragons in front of the hangars were not part of the show. Several of the military aircraft have protective barriers to prevent detailed examination, including the Avro Anson at the end of the front row, the Hawker Hurricane and Henley and Handley Page Hampden in row two, the Miles Kestrel in row three, Fairey P.4/34 at the end of row four, Armstrong Whitworth Whitley in row five then a combined fence for the Gloster F.5/34, Gladiator and Westland Lysander.

Just prior to the 1937 show and with its yellow colour scheme incomplete, the de Havilland Don was a three-seat trainer with a 525 hp D.H. Gipsy King engine; E.3 was the prototype, later becoming L2387. Fifty were ordered, thirty were delivered plus twenty unassembled or without engines. They became instructional airframes, while a few of the completed aircraft were used for communication work. L2387 became 1259M in March 1939.

Britain's latest fighter shown in 1937 was the prototype Hawker Hurricane K5083, seen here probably at Brooklands. It had made its first appearance at the previous show. Little need be said of this, one of our two most famous fighters; it passed from the makers to the A&AEE, then the RAE before becoming instructional airframe 1211M in May 1939.

Two

Into the Fifties
1946-1953

At the first post-war shows in 1946 and 1947, Britain made the most of its lead in practical jet engines, showing an Avro Lancastrian test-bed with a pair of Rolls-Royce Nenes replacing the Merlins in the outer nacelles. The Lancastrian was to prove very useful in this role and several were fitted with other types of engines.

Production jets included de Havilland Vampires, a Gloster Meteor and the prototype Supermarine E.10/44 which entered production as the Attacker, the Royal Navy's first jet fighter; de Havilland demonstrated the tail-less D.H.108 research aircraft at a time when the company was considering the layout for the forthcoming Comet jet airliner.

Britain's new airliners were the Avro Tudor and the Handey Page Hermes, neither of which was an unqualified success, but the sturdy Vickers Viking was an early success story, serving with BEA and a number of foreign airlines, while the RAF ordered the military version, the Valetta. The most successful, and smallest, of the new airliners was the de Havilland Dove, examples of which appeared at all eighteen shows between 1946 and 1964.

As the shows progressed we were to see a succession of prototypes, test-beds and experimental aircraft, with growing variants of the Gloster Meteor and de Havilland Vampire. At the same time, production began of a number of types which were to sell well, both at home and abroad; they included the Bristol Freighter, Vickers Viscount and English Electric Canberra. In the large turboprop airliner field, the Bristol Britannia appeared; biggest of all were the Bristol Brabazon and Saunders-Roe Princess flying boat, both unfortunately scrapped.

1946, and the first post-war display at the Handley Page factory airfield, Radlett. Registrations visible are Avro York G-AGOA, Lancastrian G-AHBY, Tudor G-AGRF, Lancasters G-AHJT and 'HJU of Flight Refuelling, Handley Page Halton G-AHDS, Bristol Freighter G-AHJC, Airspeed Consul G-AICZ. Smaller fry are Miles Messenger HB-EIP and Aerovan G-AIDI, Auster Autocrat G-AHSM and de Havilland Leopard Moth G-ACTJ. Fifty-seven of the sixty-one aircraft exhibited can be seen.

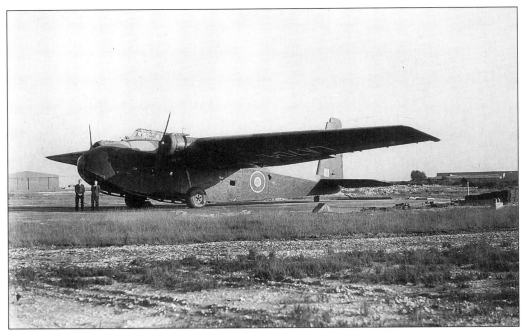

Appearing in 1946 was the General Aircraft Hamilcar X LA704, a powered version with two Bristol Mercury engines intended for the Pacific theatre where they would have been towed, as at the show, by Halifaxes. Only twenty were completed by VJ Day so this version never saw action. LA704 went to the AFEE and was SOC on 14 April 1950.

The first production de Havilland Sea Hornet F.20, TT186, flew at Hatfield on 13 August 1946 and appeared at that year's show before going to Lee-on-Solent for trials with No 703 Squadron as a long-range escort strike fighter. Three prototypes and 174 production Sea Hornets were built, not one has survived. They were powered by 2,030 hp Rolls-Royce Merlin engines.

Fairey showed the prototype Firefly Trainer in 1946, flown three months before from Ringway (now Manchester Airport). It appeared at Radlett in B Conditions marks F.1. For demonstrations abroad it became G-AHYA and several orders were secured from Canada, Ethiopia and The Netherlands. It went to the Royal Navy as MB750 in October 1947.

Also new from Fairey was the Spearfish, a two seat torpedo/dive bomber to Spec 05/43. Powered by a 2,600 hp Bristol Centaurus engine, the prototype flew before the programme was cancelled. The first, RA356, was shown at Radlett in 1946; this illustration has puzzled many as it is fitted with the wings of unbuilt Spearfish RN244!

The dragonfly-like Cierva W.9 helicopter PX203, shown in 1946, was powered by a 205 hp D.H. Gipsy Six engine whose exhaust was expelled through the tailpipe to counteract torque, thus eliminating the need for a tail rotor. Almost twenty-five per cent of engine power was absorbed by this, nearly fifty years ahead of the Hughes NOTOR (no tail rotor) helicopter. The W.9 was badly damaged on 20 January 1948, when it rolled over on take off and was not repaired.

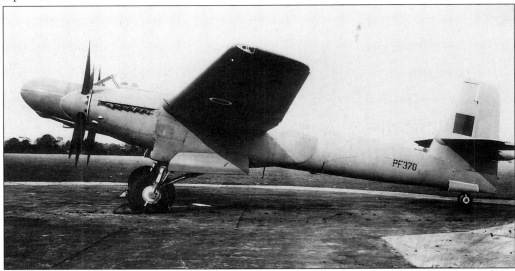

The Westland Welkin was designed to Spec F.4/40 for a single-seat high-altitude fighter to counteract the supposed threat of the high-flying bomber. Considerable problems were encountered, the threat did not materialise and PF370 was developed as a two-seat fighter. A total of seventy-seven complete Welkins plus twenty-six airframes were built, all eventually being broken up. Engines were 1,560 hp Rolls-Royce Merlins.

Prototypes of the Hawker Fury – NX802 with a Bristol Centaurus radial and VP207 with a Napier Sabre inline engine – were shown in 1947. The Centaurus version was developed into the Sea Fury, the Royal Navy's front-line carrier-based fighter, while export models went to Canada, The Netherlands, Pakistan and Egypt. Land-based Furies lacking folding wings and arrester hooks were sold to Iraq and Pakistan, while further export orders were filled from surplus Royal Navy aircraft. Total production including prototypes and two-seat trainer versions reached 883.

The prototype Handley Page Hermes II G-AGUB, shown in 1947, was powered by four 1,675 hp Bristol Hercules engines. It was contemporary of the Hastings RAF transport, of which the fourth production aircraft was also shown. G-AGUB was used for experimental work, ending its life as VX234 with the RRE at Pershore where it was scrapped in 1969. A development, the Hermes IV with 2,100 hp Hercules engines had a tricycle undercarriage; twenty-five were built, BOAC receiving twenty and Airwork five.

Successor to the Supermarine Walrus amphibian as an air-sea rescue aircraft was the Supermarine Sea Otter with a 796 hp Bristol Perseus engine mounted as a tractor in contrast to the Walrus' pusher. Total production reached 292; G-AIDM was shown in 1947 after conversion into four-passenger configuration as a demonstrator. A number of ex-Service Sea Otters were sold abroad and G-AIDM went to a customer in Venezuela as YV-P-AEN in November 1947.

In 1947, Shorts fitted a Percival Proctor with floats and it was test flown in B Conditions marks X-1. Only one was built, designated Proctor VI, and it was shown statically at Radlett before sale to Canada as CF-EHF. It was subsequently converted to a landplane.

40

The Vickers Valetta was the military version of the Viking airliner; VL249 was the prototype, seen running up its 2,000 hp Bristol Hercules engines at the 1947 show. It had made its first flight at Brooklands on 30 June. Total production amounted to 263 and Valettas replaced Dakotas in RAF Transport Command, final deliveries being made in January 1952. VL249 was sold as spares in May 1958.

A strange 1947 exhibit was the Heston AOP to Spec A.2/45; Auster submitted an aircraft to the same spec. Two Heston prototypes were built, VL529 being the first. They were powered by a 250 hp D.H. Gipsy Queen engine with a pusher propeller between the booms. The spec required as alternative float undercarriage and that the propeller could be removed for the towed flight, but the whole requirement was cancelled on 23 March 1950.

Few gliders have appeared at SBAC displays, but in 1947 Elliotts showed three and Shorts displayed the Nimbus, designed and built by two members of the company's design office. This photo, not taken at Radlett, shows it during a winch launch. A one-off, it was retired but was restored in 1985 for the Ulster Folk & Transport Museum.

Another strange shape in 1947 was the Mile Boxcar G-AJJM. With four 90 hp Blackburn Cirrus engines, it was a derivative of the Aerovan. The detachable hold – the dark area in the photograph – could be pre-loaded and was roadable. After removal of the hold, the rear fuselage was brought forward to link with the nose section. The project came to nothing and G-AJJM was scrapped in 1948.

Designed as a replacement for the Blackburn Firebrand, the company's submission to Spec S.28/43 was the powerful-looking B-48 with a 2,475 hp Bristol Centaurus engine. RT651 was the only prototype completed of two ordered, but one example of a modified version was built. Advent of the turboprop killed the project.

A general view of the 1947 show; in the foreground the two Hawker Furies, NX802 and VP207, two-seat Spitfire G-AIDN and Sea Otter G-AIDM with the heavier metal beyond. The Spitfire was a conversion of Mk VIII MT818 and was used as a demonstrator; around thirty such conversions were made of Mk IXs for overseas customers. G-AIDN is still airworthy and flies under US ownership in Oregon as MT818.

The attractive little Reid & Sigrist R.S.3 Desford G-AGOS with 130 hp D.H. Gipsy Major engines was a tandem-seat trainer. Shown in 1946 and 1947, it attracted no orders but was later modified to include a prone pilot's position in the nose for research into this aspect which was to come to fruition in the 1954 prone pilot Meteor. The Desford survives in its modified form serialled VZ724 and designated R.S.4 Bobsleigh.

Contrasting with the Sea Otter (page 40), Supermarine showed the first of three Attacker prototypes, TS409, powered with a 5,000 lb thrust Rolls-Royce Nene turbojet. It became the Royal Navy's first jet fighter; of 185 built, 149 went to the Navy and thirty-six to the Pakistan Air Force.

Following its damage at Brussels in 1947, the Gloster Meteor IV demonstrator G-AIDC was used as the basis for the two-seat demonstrator G-AKPK with 3,500 lb thrust Rolls-Royce Derwents. Its brilliant red and ivory scheme became well known and an RAF order for T.7 trainers was secured. G-AKPK was sold to the Royal Netherlands Air Force in November 1948 as I-1.

The show moved to its present home, Farnborough in 1948 with a whole rash of new types. The smallest helicopter exhibited was the Cierva Skeeter 1 G-AJCJ with a 110 hp Jameson engine. It first flew at Southampton Airport the following month and was used for test flying, being broken up there in November 1952. More powerful Skeeters served with Britain's Army Air Corps, the German Army and Navy and the Portuguese Air Force.

A non-flyer at Farnborough – or anywhere else – was the four-seat Planet Satellite. Built of magnesium alloy and with a retractable undercarriage, it was powered by a 250 hp D.H. Gipsy Queen engine driving a pusher propeller behind the V-tail. An interesting concept, ahead of its time, it had an estimated maximum speed of 208 mph; attempts to fly at Blackbushe were abandoned and it was melted down at Redhill in 1958. The fuselage of a second Satellite was used in the Firth helicopter which was also unsuccessful.

A view from the control tower in 1948. In the foreground, the second Miles Marathon G-AILH, a production Handley Page Hastings TG527 and, in the second row, Bristol Freighter G-AIFO, Brigand RH809 and Short Sealand G-AIVX. Readers who have attended the Farnborough shows will recognise this area as being on the opposite side of the runway to later events.

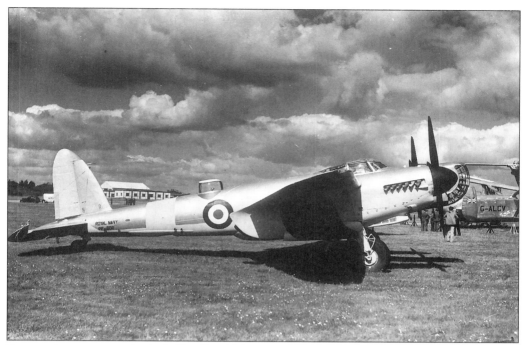

Seen against a stormy sky is de Havilland Mosquito TT.39 PF606, one of twenty-six converted by General Aircraft involving an ugly extended nose and dorsal observation dome to meet a Royal Navy requirement for a target tug. It was also used for radar calibration until being SOC at Lossiemouth on 27 November 1952.

Designed as a replacement for the Sea Otter as an air-sea rescue aircraft, the Supermarine Seagull amphibian had a 1,815 hp Rolls-Royce Griffon engine driving contra-rotating propellers. Two prototypes were completed, PA143 and '147; this is the first but the type never entered production and the two, plus a third uncompleted airframe, PA152, were sold for scrap in 1952.

Handley Page presented the twenty-ninth production Hastings transport, TG527, and the first RAF squadron to equip with the type was No 47 at Dishforth in September 1948 – this was one of the aircraft which went to that unit. It served for twenty years, its last operator being the SCBS before being SOC on 4 November 1968.

Two Armstong Whitworth AW.52 flying wings were built for research, following a small glider, the AW52G RG324 shown at the 1946 event. TS363 with two 5,000 lb Rolls-Royce Nene turbojets was followed by TS368 with 3,500 lb Rolls-Royce Derwents – the former is illustrated. Both appeared at the 1948 show; TS363 suffered flutter on 30 May 1949 and the pilot, J.O. Lancaster, became the first UK pilot to use a Martin-Baker ejector seat in an emergency. Oddly, the aircraft glided down and landed in open country with little damage. TS368 went to RAE Farnborough until disposal in June 1954.

48

Glider manufacturer Elliotts of Newbury showed their one-off four-seat Newbury Eon G-AKBC in 1947, with a 100 hp Blackburn Cirrus Minor engine and again in 1948, this time re-engined with a 145 hp D.H. Gipsy Major. Used by the company as a glider tug it was a familiar sight in this role until 14 April 1950 when attempting a pilotless take-off at Lympne with a glider in tow! Both went through the airfield hedge, fortunately without casualties.

Developed from the smaller Percival Merganser shown in 1947, the prototype Prince, G-ALCM appeared in 1948. Originally powered by 520 hp Alvis Leonides engines, later versions had 560 hp Leonides. A successful light transport, it notched up a considerable number of orders for various models from civil and military customers at home and abroad, almost 170 being built. G-ALCM was dismantled at its birthplace, Luton, in July 1956.

An abiding memory for anyone attending the 1948 show must be the inverted fly-past by Geoffrey Tyson in the Saunders-Roe SR.A/1 TG271. Designed as a fighter flying boat to operate in the Pacific, it had two Metropolitan-Vickers Beryl jet engines which, in the three prototypes, ranged from 3,230 lb to 3,850 lb thrust. TG267 and '271 were both lost in 1949 in accidents but TG263 survives in the Southampton Hall of Aviation.

Designed to Spec T.7/45 for a Percival Prentice replacement as the RAF's basic trainer, the Avro Athena and Boulton-Paul Balliol were both originally designed for turbine power. Prototypes were built with Armstrong Siddeley Mamba and Rolls-Royce Dart turboprops but changing requirements and non- availability of the turbines led to redesign of both to take the 1,280 hp Rolls-Royce Merlin. The Balliol won the major contract but shown is the first of four Athena T.2 prototypes, VW890. Only fifteen were built, replacing the North American Harvard for armament training at the RAF Flying College, Manby.

Contrasting with the Skeeter (page 45), Cierva's Air Horse G-ALCV was Britain's largest helicopter with three rotors driven via a gearbox by a single 1,620 hp Rolls-Royce Merlin engine. It was shown statically in 1948, making its first flight at Southampton Airport on 7 December 1948 as VZ724. The first of two, it crashed on 13 June 1950 due to hub fatigue, killing the crew. The second Air Horse, G-ALCW, was flown as WA555 and later stored.

A nice spread of types at the 1949 show. It is obviously not practicable to identify everything, but prominent among the airliners are prototypes of the de Havilland Comet G-ALVG, Armstrong Whitworth Apollo G-AIYN, Vickers Viscount G-AHRF and Handley Page Hermes 5 G-ALEU. The last named is behind the Viscount and next to the first production Hermes 4, G-ALDA. At bottom left is the prototype English Electric Canberra, VN799. The mighty Brabazon G-AGPW flew past but did not land (see page 57).

The prototype de Havilland Comet 1 G-ALVG comes in to land after its first SBAC appearance in 1949. The large single main wheels were replaced in production aircraft with a bogie undercarriage. G-ALVG was broken up at Farnborough in July 1953.

If the Comet was 1949's civilian star, the prototype English Electric Canberra bomber VN799 in an all-blue scheme was undoubtedly the military highlight, displayed, as many Canberras were later, by Roland Beamont. Replacing other bombers in RAF service, various Canberra versions equipped sixty-one squadrons and achieved a number of export orders. UK production reached almost 950, while Martin built the type under licence in the USA as the B-57.

Basically a swept-wing version of the Attacker, the Supermarine 510 VV106 was powered by a 5,000 lb Rolls-Royce Nene and was built to investigate flight behaviour at high sub-sonic speeds. It paved the way for the Supermarine 535 and 541 tricycle undercarriage developments which in turn led to the Swift. Behind, also making its SBAC debut, the prototype Vickers Viscount, destined to become Britain's best-ever selling airliner and the world's first turbine powered airliner with its four 1,380 ehp Rolls-Royce Darts.

Lt Cdr Mike Lithgow with the Supermarine 510 VV106 which he flew at the 1949 show. He was to recapture the world's absolute speed record in 1953 of 722.6 mph set nineteen days previously by Neville Duke in a modified Hawker Hunter. However, Lithgow's new record – 737.7 mph set in a Supermarine Swift in Tripoli - lasted nine days before being recaptured by the USA.

Developed from the Vickers Viking and Valetta, the prototype Varsity trainer VX828 appeared in 1949. Powered by 1,950 hp Bristol Hercules engines, it had a tricycle undercarriage and a fixed ventral pannier for the bomb aimer and practice bombs. Production totalled 163 and Varsities replaced Wellingtons and Valettas.

A spirited display in 1950 by the first Vickers Viscount 700 G-AMAV, typical of the initial production series of the world's first turboprop airliner. Powered with Rolls-Royce Darts from 1,740 to 1,990 ehp, depending on the variant, around 450 Viscounts were built and the type served throughout the world. G-AMAV remained with the manufacturer for extensive test flying until its withdrawal from use at Wisley in 1961, the fuselage going to Stansted in August 1963.

The elegant Airspeed Ambassador was a forty-seven-seat airliner powered by 2,625 hp Bristol Centaurus engines. The second prototype, G-AKRD, was shown in 1950, having appeared at the two previous events. Following two prototypes and one pre-production aircraft, twenty were built for British European Airways. By 1957 they were being replaced by Viscounts and were sold to other British and foreign airlines. G-AKRD went to Rolls-Royce as an engine test-bed (see page 121).

Making its show debut in 1950 was WE530, the second prototype Percival Provost. It was the winner in a contest to provide a replacement for the Prentice as the RAF's basic trainer, the loser being the very similar Handley Page H.P.R.2, also shown that year. Powered by a 550 hp Alvis Leonides engine, 388 Provosts were built and Percival achieved some export success with armed versions.

Armstrong Whitworth showed their Apollo turboprop airliner G-AIYN in 1949, '50 and '51 before conceding defeat to the Viscount. Two Apollos were built with Armstrong Siddeley Mamba engines but no orders were received. Both were transferred to military marks; G-AIYN became VX220 and was broken up at its birthplace, Coventry's Baginton airport, in 1955.

The de Havilland Venom N.F.2 night fighter prototype appeared in 1950 in B Conditions marks G-5-3 and later became WP227. Total production of all marks of Venom reached 1,143, of which some 385 were two-seaters, including Sea Venoms for the Royal Navy and Royal Australian Navy. The two-seat night fighters were also built for Sweden and licence production took place in France as the Aquilon. Venoms were powered by a single de Havilland Ghost turbojet of 4,850 to 5,300 lb thrust, depending on variant. WP227 went to the A&AEE, eventually becoming instructional airframe 7098M.

The Bristol Brabazon G-AGPW, the largest landplane built in Britain, made its first SBAC appearance in 1949, flying in each day from its base at Filton, Bristol but not landing at Farnborough. For the next two events it was based at Farnborough; here it is landing at Filton. Eight 2,500 hp Bristol Centaurus engines coupled in pairs drove contra-rotating propellers giving a speed of 300 mph. A second aircraft was partly built, but both were broken up in October 1953.

1951 and the Bristol Brabazon dominates the scene. Beyond are the Avro Shackleton WB822, Ashton WB491, English Electric Canbarras WD935 and VX185, Short Sperrin VX158 and Vickers Viscount G-AMAV. The exhibition tent is in the distance, head-on.

First of a long line – the Hawker P.1067 prototype WB188 in 1951; in production it became the Hunter. The majority of the 1,972 built were powered by Rolls-Royce Avons with thrust from 7,700 to 10,150 lb, but the 150 Mk 2s and 5s had the Armstrong Siddeley Sapphire giving 8,000 lb. There were many export customers for new and refurbished aircraft. WB188 in slightly modified form set a new world speed record of 722.6 mph in 1953 and is preserved in the Tangmere Military Aviation Museum.

Predecessor of the Hawker P.1067 was the P.1052, VX272, the second of which, VX279, had appeared at the 1949 show. On completion of its test programme, VX272 became instructional airframe 7174M while VX279 was converted to the P.1081. Both were powered by a 5,000 lb Rolls-Royce Nene turbojet.

In 1950, Gloster built as a private venture a ground attack version of the Meteor 8. Shown statically at that year's event, it was registered G-AMCJ. In 1951, repainted silver with B Conditions marks G-7-1 and with twenty-four rockets plus wing tip tanks it was spectacularly demonstrated by Jan Zurakowski, performing one-and-a-half vertical cartwheels, a highlight of the flying display.

The prototype Vickers Valiant WB210 landing at the 1951 show. First of the three V-bombers, it was lost in an in-flight fire the following January but 107 were built between 1949 and 1957 to equip ten squadrons and No 232 Operational Conversion Unit. Valiant XD818 which dropped Britain's first H-bomb at Christmas Island on 15 May 1957 is preserved in the RAF Museum, Hendon.

The second Supermarine 508 VX136 shows off its folding wings on the runway in 1952. Powered by two Rolls-Royce AJ.65s, later developed as Avons, of 6,500 lb thrust, it provided useful data for the swept-wing Supermarine 525 which in turn was developed into the Scimitar.

A rather scattered static park in 1952. Among the larger exhibits can be seen a pair of de Havilland Comets, G-ALVG and CF-CUM, prototypes of the Blackburn & General Aircraft Universal Freighter WF320, Bristol Britannia G-ALBO, Short Sperrin VX158 and Avro Shackleton MR.2 WG531. The Bristol Freighter next to the Canadian Comet is NZ5906 for the Royal New Zealand Air Force.

The Saunders-Roe Princess impressed by its sheer size in 1952 and flew over daily from Cowes. G-ALUN was the only one of three completed; it weighed 100 tons, was powered by ten Bristol Proteus turbines in four pairs with contra-props and two single outer engines. Each engine developed 2,500 shp and the cruising speed at 37,000 ft was 380 mph. The venture came to nothing; various schemes fell through and G-ALUN made its last show appearance in 1953. All three were broken up at Southampton in 1965-66.

The prototype Avro 698 VX770, subsequently named Vulcan, appeared in 1952 only three days after its first flight, flown solo by Roly Falk who at the time had only flown it for two hours. The giant white triangle was accompanied by an Avro 707A and 707B – small scale models of the big design. Three years later at Farnborough Falk rolled the second production Vulcan – a sight to be seen! The Vulcan remained a favourite at air shows until the RAF retired its last example. VX770 had four 6,500 lb Rolls-Royce Avons, while later production models had Bristol Siddeley Olympus ranging from 11,000 to 20,000 lb.

Another delta to appear in 1952 was the second prototype Gloster Javelin, WD808, the RAF's new all-weather fighter. Unlike the Vulcan, it had a tailplane, also of delta configuration. Seven prototypes and 428 production Javelins of eight variants were built between 1956 and 1959, the last production versions being the Mk 8. No 64 Squadron in Singapore was the last Javelin unit, disbanding in June 1967, WD808 was lost in a crash at Flax Bourton, near Bristol on 28 May 1953.

The third prototype Fairey Gannet anti-submarine aircraft, WE488, was shown in 1951 and 1952. Its Armstrong Siddeley Double Mamba turboprop drove contra-rotating propellers and the two coupled engines enabled it to cruise on one and feather the other propeller. Total Gannet production reached 274, including three prototypes; overseas sales were to West Germany, Australia and Indonesia. WE488 was damaged beyond repair at Edinburgh/Turnhouse on 9 October 1953.

Seen in boisterous mood in 1952 was the Westland Dragonfly WG707. A licence-built Sikosky S-51 with modifications to British requirements, 149 Dragonflys were built for the Royal Navy and RAF, civilian operators and for export. Some were later converted to Widgeons with a re-designed front fuselage to accommodate an extra passenger. All versions were powered by a 520 hp Alvis Leonides piston engine.

Largest of Britain's post-war propeller-driven airliners to enter production was the Bristol Britannia; G-ALBO, the prototype was shown in 1952, powered by 2,800 ehp Bristol Proteus turbines. It had 3,780 ehp Proteus by the time it appeared in the 1953 show. Including prototypes, eighty-two Britannias of various types were built, serving with BOAC and other airlines, while twenty-three went to the RAF. G-ALBO became instructional airframe 7708M from October 1960 at RAF St Athan.

Another Bristol debutante in 1952 was the Type 173 helicopter G-ALBN. Seating thirteen passengers, it had two 850 hp Alvis Leonides Major engines with rotor gearboxes interconnected enabling one engine to drive both rotors in the event of failure. Considerable test flying took place with five aircraft leading to the Type 192 which emerged as the Belvedere for the RAF, by which time Bristol had become part of the Westland company. Like many other aircraft, G-ALBN finished up as an instructional airframe, 7648M.

The Scottish Aviation Prestwick Pioneer had been seen at previous SBAC events with a D.H. Gipsy Queen engine. By 1952 it had an Alvis Leonides with 520 or 560 hp, depending on the variant, in production aircraft. Registered G-AKBF, it gave an impressive display of short take-off and landings, even though the port half of the elevator was torn away on take-off! Fifty-nine Pioneers were built and served with the RAF overseas, while four went to the Royal Ceylon Air Force and nine to the Royal Malayan Air Force. G-AKBF went to the RAF as XE612.

Part of a research programme into delta-wing dynamics was the little Boulton-Paul BP.111 VT935 powered by a 5,100 lb Rolls-Royce Nene. It had appeared in 1951 in a silver scheme but after three accidents was modified as the BP.111A and painted bright yellow as seen here in 1953. On completion of its test programme it was donated to the Cranfield College of Aeronautics and is now preserved at the Midland Air Museum at Coventry Airport.

The de Havilland Dove light transport first flew in September 1945 and was an immediate success. Early models had 300 hp D.H Gipsy Queen engines but later production aircraft had 400 hp Gipsy Queens. More than 520 Doves were built and sold throughout the world to civil and military customers. The type was seen at every SBAC show from 1946 to 1964. Illustrated is Dove 6 G-AMZM which appeared without a break from 1953 to 1959. It was sold to Sweden in May 1972 as SE-GRA and is still currently registered there.

Demonstrating its ability to fly on one engine while carrying an airborne lifeboat is Avro Shackleton MR.2 WL796. The growl of a Shackleton's four 2,450 hp Rolls-Royce Griffons driving contra-props is still remembered with affection by Shackleton buffs. Total production of all marks was 188 plus three prototypes. Included were eight MR.3s with tricycle undercarriage supplied to the South African Air Force. WL793 was eventually converted to AEW.2 standard and last flew with No 8 Squadron before becoming instructional airframe 8675M.

Hidden away on the far side of the airfield during the 1953 show were three V-bomber prototypes – Avro Vulcans VX770 and '777 plus the Handley Page Victor WB771. All were confined to this paddock until they took part in the flying display, after which they returned to the corral. One never knew what prying eyes might discover about our latest weapons!

66

Exciting comment in 1953 was the sole Vickers Valiant B.2 WJ954. Designed as a low-level bomber with a strengthened structure in the normal wheel well area, this version had pods into which the main wheels retracted. It had the same 10,000 lb Rolls-Royce Avons as the B.1. When these Valiants assumed a low-level role in 1964 they lasted less than a year before metal fatigue in the wing spars caused withdrawal from service – one wonders if the B.2 would have survived longer in this role?

In 1947 the first Commonwealth-built aircraft to appear at a SBAC show was the Chipmunk. In 1953, from the same stable, was the de Havilland Canada Beaver. G-ANAR was the only Mk 2 built and differed from standard in having a modified fin and rudder plus a 550 hp Alvis Leonides engine. Shown as a demonstrator at six shows between 1953 and 1960, it attracted no orders and returned to Canada as CF-CNR in August 1971.

The Boulton-Paul Balliol won the contract for an RAF basic trainer (see notes on the Avro Athena, page 50). In addition to eight prototypes, 145 production production aircraft were built. The first entered RAF service in February 1952 and the last was delivered in April 1954. The final six were withdrawn in 1961. Twelve were supplied to the Royal Ceylon Air Force and the Royal Navy received thirty Sea Balliols with certain undercarriage modifications and arrester hooks for deck-landing training - WL715, shown in 1953, was the first of these.

Something different in 1953 was the Bristol Freighter G-AINL displaying the fuselage of Supermarine Attacker WK337 in its hold. On the left is the Blackburn Universal Freighter WZ889, production versions of which were to become the Beverley. G-AINL had a varied career, serving for two periods as WJ320, went to Eire for eight months in 1952 as EI-AFP and was eventually sold to Canada in November 1968 as CF-YDO.

Three

Jets Supreme
1954-1960

As the shows proceeded through the fifties, so the jet engine made its presence more and more felt (and heard!). Most impressive sight at the 1953 event was the two Avro Vulcan prototypes in formation with four Avro 707 research deltas, built as scale models of the big bomber. At this time, sonic booms were all the rage – they were later banned when a fast run by an English Electric Lightning allegedly broke windows in the control tower!

Britain's third V-bomber, the Handley Page Victor, made its appearance and throughout this period Hawker Hunters were seen in profusion, not only as company demonstrators but as RAF aerobatic teams, most famous of which were No 92 Squadron's Blue Diamonds and No 111's Black Arrows which set the standard for all such teams. In 1958, the Service participation included two large formations of Hunters and Javelins, forty-five of each.

As the show entered the sixties it was opened each day by a V-bomber scramble, Taking turns, they included four Valiants of No 148 Squadron, four Vulcans from No 617 (the Dam Busters) and four Victors from No 15.

For the first time, foreign engines were admitted in British airframes, but these aircraft could not be included in the flying programme (nobody has yet explained how the Fairey Fantome with a Hispano-Suiza engine was allowed to fly at the 1935 show!).

We only showed the nose of a Bristol Freighter opposite so here, in 1954, is a military version, the Mk 31M in B Conditions marks G-18-166, intended for the Pakistan Air Force who received thirty-eight of this version plus thirty-four of the earlier Mk 21s, thereby becoming by far the largest operator of the type. The Mk 31M had 1,980 hp Bristol Hercules engines; this particular aircraft became PAF S4426.

Lined up in the 1954 static park were three Gloster Javelin prototypes, WT827, '830 and '836 plus the first and third Javelin FAW.1s, XA544 and '546. These early aircraft had two 8,000 lb Armstrong Siddeley Sapphire engines. Fates recorded are WT830 to A&AEE then 7485M, WT836 to A&AEE then 7552M, XA544 to 7558M while XA546 was lost and the RAE pilot killed when it crashed on 21 October 1954 in the Bristol Channel.

Pilots who took the five Javelins to Farnborough in 1954 were, left to right: F/Lt Webster, Peter Varley, Geoff Worrall, S/Ldr P. Scott, F/Lt A. Jeffries (navigator) and Dicky Martin, Gloster's chief test pilot, Javelins.

Forerunner of many Folland Gnats was the lower-powered Midge G-39-1, flown at the 1954 show with verve by Folland's test pilot 'Ted' Tennant. Powered by a 1,640 lb Armstrong Siddeley Viper, it was claimed to have a maximum speed of more than 600 mph. The Midge crashed at Chilbolton on 26 September 1955.

Another small aircraft shown in 1954 was the Fairey F.D.1, VX350, built for research initially into vertical take-off from a ramp, but following test with models the idea was abandoned and the F.D.1 was used to investigate stability and rolling performance of delta shapes and use of braking parachutes. Powered by a 3,600 lb Rolls-Royce Derwent, it was written off on 6 February 1956 in an emergency landing after which it was sent to the Proof & Experimental Establishment at Shoeburyness for destruction.

The Scottish Aviation Twin Pioneer was a remarkable STOL performer. Shown in 1955 was the prototype, G-ANTP, powered by 540 hp Alvis Leonides engines. Later versions had 560 or 640 hp Leonides, or 600 hp Pratt & Whitney Wasps. Eighty-seven were built and served with both civil and military operators, thirty-nine going to the RAF. G-ANTP was lost in a take-off crash in Assam on 10 March 1960.

The Short S.B.5 WG768, shown first in 1954, was built for low-speed trials of the swept-wing configuration of the English Electric P.1 developed as the Lightning. Only one S.B.1 was built but a number of wing sweep and tailplane positions were tried – this photo show it with a sixty degree sweep and tailplane on top of the fin. By 1954 the tailplane had been moved to below the fuselage. At this time the S.B.1 was powered by a 3,500 lb Rolls-Royce Derwent. The aircraft is preserved in the Cosford Aerospace Museum.

Like its stablemate the Dove, de Havilland's Heron was present in various guises at a number of SBAC shows without break from 1950 to 1960. G-ANCJ was a Mk 2 with 250 hp D.H. Gipsy Queen engines, flying comfortably here on two. Including prototypes, 149 Herons were built for civil and military customers worldwide. G-ANCJ was sold to the Leeward Islands as VP-LIB in January 1960.

Another Short research aircraft shown in 1954 was the S.B.4 Sherpa, designed to investigate the aeroisoclinic wing which would overcome loss of incidence in swept wings under bending loads. Originally flown as the S.B.1 glider, it was rebuilt following a crash and fitted with two 353 lb Blackburn-Turboméca Palas turbojets. After providing useful data the Sherpa was retired and passed through several hands; at the time of writing it was being restored to static display condition by the Royal Aeronautical Society branch at Rochester.

Many VIPs have visited the shows; here on 6 September 1955, Lord and Lady Trenchard chat with Air Chief Marshal Sir Francis Fogarty and Sir Roy Dobson who had become Managing Director of Avro in 1941. In 1958 he became Managing Director of the Hawker Siddeley Group and its Chairman in 1963.

Third of the V-bombers was the Handley Page Victor; in 1953 the first prototype was shown, while in 1954 and '55 the second, WB775, was seen, the first having been destroyed in a crash at Cranfield on 14 July 1954 when a fatigue failure removed the tailplane. Both prototypes were powered by four 8,000 lb Armstrong Siddeley Sapphires. WB775 was dismantled and components taken to the RAE to investigate the cause of the crash of the first Victor B.2, XH668, on 20 August 1959.

Short's Seamew was a two-seat lightweight anti-submarine aircraft with a 1,320 shp Armstrong Siddeley Mamba turboprop – the second prototype XA213 seen here had a 1,590 shp Mamba. Four Seamews were exhibited in 1955; the programme was cancelled in 1957 in an economy drive after twenty-four were built.

Although fixed-wing aircraft are not permitted to fly in to Farnborough during the period of the exhibition because they would have to approach over parked aircraft in the static, a number of visitors arrive by helicopter. Here, the Prime Minister, The Rt Hon Sir Anthony Eden, deplanes on 6 September 1955 from a Westland Dragonfly.

The Westland Widgeon was a private venture by the company and was a conversion of the Westland-Sikorsky WS-51 featuring a wider forward fuselage to accommodate an extra seat and WS-55 rotor components with shortened blades. G-ALIK was the first conversion, shown in 1955. Powerplant was a 520 hp Alvis Leonides; three Widgeons were converted from WS-51s and twelve production aircraft were built of which six were exported and five served with Bristow Helicopters. G-ALIK was re-registered G-APPS before sale to Trinidad as VP-TCM in December 1962.

Jan Zurakowski, remembered for his brilliant flying in the P.V. Meteor in 1951 (see page 59) had subsequently gone to Avro Canada and in 1955 demonstrated their CF-100-4B 18321 in another supreme display culminating in a falling leaf. Total production of all variants of the CF-100 including prototypes reached 691, mostly for the Royal Canadian Air Force but fifty-three were supplied to Belgium. The Mk 4B illustrated was powered by two 7,300 lb Avro Canada Orenda engines.

On 10 March 1956, Britain regained the world's speed record when Peter Twiss flying the Fairey F.D.2 research aircraft reached 1,132 mph over a course between Ford and Chichester – an increase of 310 mph. Two F.D.2s were built, WG774 and '777; the former, with its record noted beneath the cockpit, is towed into position at the 1956 show with RAE technician Norman Parker in the cockpit. Powerplant was a 10,000 lb Rolls-Royce Avon. WG774 was subsequently fitted with a new ogival wing and other modifications for Concorde development work; it is preserved along with a Concorde prototype in the Fleet Air Arm Museum, Yeovilton.

Peter Twiss with his wife, plus Fairey's Chief Test Pilot Gordon Slade and his wife inspect the record-breaking F.D.2. The nose forward of the cockpit canopy could be lowered for take-off and landing to improve forward visibility – a system later used in Concorde.

Part of the 1956 static park; in the foreground Supermarine Swift F.7 XF113 with Swift FR.5 WK296 beyond. Twelve F.7s were built for guided missile development, equipping No 1 Guided Weapon Development Squadron at Valley, Anglesey from December 1956 until withdrawal from service with No 2 and 79 Squadrons in Germany from February 1956 to March 1961. WK296 was SOC on 19 September 1961.

The prototype Hawker Hunter F.6 XF833 flew on 23 January 1954 but suffered a number of engine problems with its 10,000 lb Rolls-Royce Avon. After prototype trials had been completed it was fitted with an experimental Rolls-Royce thrust-reversal system incorporating exhaust louvres beneath the tailplane and appeared at the 1956 show.

Hawker showed no less than six Hunters in 1956; here, five are seen on their way to Farnborough. In the lead is Bill Bedford in the T.7 XJ615, without roundels is F.4 XF310 with Fireflash missiles flown by Duncan Simpson, Frank Bullen flew tip-tanked F.6 XG131, Hugh Mereweather F.6 XG129 with four under-wing tanks and David Lockspeiser is bringing up the rear in F.6 XG128 with tanks and rockets.

The Hunter pilots, from left to right: Frank Bullen, Bill Bedford, Duncan Simpson, Hugh Mereweather and David Lockspeiser. The reason why Duncan wore dark overalls was that he had been soaked in kerosene while carrying out an external check on a Hunter when it was being refuelled!

One of several demonstrations at the shows, seen here in 1957, when a Fairey Ultra-light helicopter landed on the back of a moving lorry representing a ship's landing platform. Six Ultra-lights were built, five flew and one was used for ground tests. Powered by a 252 lb Blackburn-Turboméca Palouste which supplied compressed air to pressure burners on the rotor tips, the design requirement was for an easily dismantleable and cheap helicopter for army work. In spite of impressive demonstrations no orders were placed and the programme ended in 1959. G-AOUK was the fourth built and was formerly serialled XJ926.

A queue to see the interior of the fourth Vickers Viscount 803 for KLM, PH-VID *Otto Lilenthal*, in 1957. The Dutch airline bought nine Viscounts and when they were replaced in the mid-1960s by DC-9s, sold them to Aer Lingus.

Monday morning at the 1957 show was wet! The Aviation Traders Accountant G-ATEL was the prototype of a twenty-eight passenger airliner powered by 1,740 ehp Rolls-Royce Dart turboprops. Behind the project was Freddie Laker whose name was later to become synonymous with cheaper airline fares. Unfortunately no backers or customers could be found and it was eventually broken up at Southend in February 1960.

The French company Hurel-Dubois, noted for high aspect ratio wing design, collaborated with Miles in 1957 to produced a wing for experimental flying on Aerovan VI G-AJOF, in which form it was designated HDM.105. Re-registered G-AHDM, it appeared at the 1957 show; this photo, taken shortly before its re-registration, barely shows B Conditions marks G-35-3. The project was scrapped when it was damaged beyond repair at Shoreham on 28 June 1958. Forty-eight standard Aerovans were built; 'HDM had 155 hp Blackburn Cirrus Major engines.

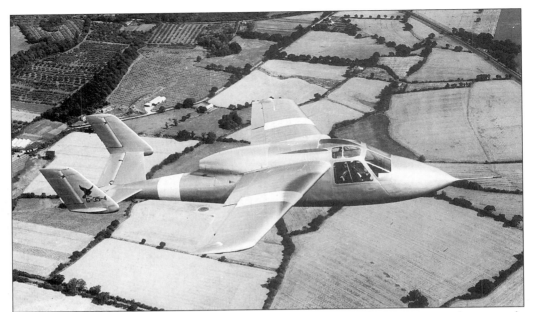

Built as a private venture, the Miles Student was an all-metal jet trainer with a tricycle undercarriage, powered by a 880 lb Turboméca Marbore engine. Miles hoped to persuade the RAF that its purchase and operating costs would be much less than the Jet Provost, but with limited resources prototype manufacture took too long and the RAF decision had been made. Initial B Conditions marks G-35-4 were later changed to G-APLK, then military marks XS941. Following a crash on 24 August 1985 the remains have been stored.

The mixed powerplant Saunder-Roe SR.53 research aircraft had one 8,000 lb de Havilland Spectre rocket motor above which was a 1,640 lb Armstrong Siddeley Viper. The two prototypes, XD145 and '151, were shown in 1957, the latter statically. They provided useful information for the proposed SR.177 fighter which unfortunately was not built. XD151 was destroyed in a fatal crash at Boscombe Down on 15 June 1958 while XD145 is preserved at the Cosford Aerospace Museum.

The second production Handley Page Victor B.1 XA918 with everything down in 1957 – photographers are not allowed this close to the runway now! Waiting its turn to take off is the second prototype Vulcan VX777 modified as the B.2 aerodynamic airframe. Victor B.1s had four 11,050 lb Armstrong Siddeley Sapphire turbojets and entered service in November 1957. Total B.1 production was fifty; XA918 was the first of a a number converted to BK.1 tankers.

Biggest Westland helicopter was the private venture Westminster heavy-lift transport. Two versions were projected – a forty-seat short range civil transport and a flying crane capable of lifting up to 15,000 lb. G-APLE was basically a flying test rig with two 2,920 shp Napier Eland turboshafts, it appeared in the 1958 show and in 1959 when it was joined by a second, G-APTX. In spite of an impressive performance the programme was abandoned in September 1960 and both were cut up for scrap.

In 1958, borrowing several aircraft from other squadrons, the RAF *Black Arrows* aerobatic team led by Sqn Ldr Roger Topp looped twenty-two Hunters in formation – the biggest number of aircraft to carry out this manoeuvre. The Pakistan Air Force had looped twenty-one earlier in the year.

A modification of the Chipmunk by de Havilland in 1958 was the Mk 23, a single-seat crop duster with built-in wingtip slots and a raised cockpit. The second aircraft, evaluated by Fison-Airwork, was G-APOS, seen with its hopper being refilled, engine running, on the Farnborough runway. Several others were converted by Farm Aviation who had acquired G-APOS, which was sold to USA as N8345 in August 1968.

An important new type in 1958 was the Blackburn NA.39, prototype of the Buccaneer. The nearest two aircraft, XK486 and '487, were shown at Farnborough. They were the first and second prototypes – also in the picture is the fifth, XK490. These aircraft had two 7,000 lb D.H. Gyron Junior turbojets, like the Buccaneer S.1.

A far cry in 1958 from the prototype de Havilland Comet displayed in 1949 was the first Mk 4, G-APDA, for BOAC to whom it was delivered on 24 February 1959. It subsequently served with Malaysian Airways from November 1965 as 9M-AOA, passed to Malaysia-Singapore Airlines in March 1966 as 9M-BAS and returned to Gatwick in November 1969. By 1972 it had been reduced to spares at Lasham. Comet 4s had four 10,500 lb Rolls-Royce Avon turbojets.

Appearing at the 1958 and 1959 shows was the Fairey Rotodyne XE521 which gave an impressive demonstration of what a vertical take-off airliner could be. Powered by two 2,800 shp Napier Eland turboprops which drove the propellers and provided power for tip jets on the rotor blades, it was extremely noisy but a brilliant concept. Unfortunately, in spite of initial interest by BEA and several foreign operators, the programme was cancelled in February 1962 following Westland's take over of Fairey.

First shown in 1958 was the Short S.C.1 XG900, while in 1959 the second aircraft, XG905, appeared. Powered by five 2,000 lb Rolls-Royce RB.108 engines, one for horizontal flight and four for vertical lift, it was Britain's first fixed-wing VTO aircraft providing valuable data for this type of operation. Its demonstration was cut short when grass was ingested into the air intakes – a crew member at the rear appears to be holding some grass. Both S.C.1s are preserved, XG900 with the Fleet Air Arm Museum, Yeovilton and '905 at the Ulster Folk and Transport Museum.

Lowest fly past at any SBAC show came in 1959 with the Saunders-Roe SR.N1 hovercraft G-12-4, pioneer of the large hovercraft to come from the company and which are still operating in the UK and overseas. Powered by a 435 hp Alvis Leonides engine, the SR.N1 is shown about to embark twenty Royal Marines for a trip down the runway.

A VIP visitor in 1959 was Admiral of the Fleet Lord Louis Mountbatten, shown in the cockpit of the SR.N1. On 25 July of that year, the hovercraft made the Channel crossing between Calais and Dover, celebrating the fiftieth anniversary of Bleriot's crossing.

Something which the CAA would certainly not allow today – Supermarine Scimitars XD267/193 and XD248/195 landed from the the west and folded their wings while XD244/191 landed between them! All were from No 807 Squadron based at Lossiemouth before joining HMS *Ark Royal* in March 1960 for the Mediterranean. Scimitars had two 10,000 lb Rolls-Royce Avon engines.

The 1959 aircraft park with a wide variety of types. In the foreground are the Napier de-icing trials Avro Lincoln G-APRJ, Armstrong Whitworth Argosy G-APVH, Vickers Viscount VH-TVR, D.H. Heron G-APEV and Dove G-AMZN, Percival President G-APVJ which was removed before the public days and Scottish Aviation Twin Pioneer XM958. On the runway are Avro Vulcan B.2 XH536, Handley Page Herald G-AODF, Fairey Rotodyne XE521, Vickers Vanguard G-APEB, Armstrong Whitworth Argosy G-APRN and de Havilland Comet 4b G-APMB.

A natural development of the Bristol 173 (see page 64) was the 192, of which nine pre-production examples were built – XG451 was the fifth, seen in 1959 with non-standard spats on the rear wheels. Powered by two 1,465 hp Napier Gazelles, it is carrying a Bristol Bloodhound surface-to-air missile. In production form the 192 became the Westland Belvedere (Westland having taken over Bristol) and the RAF received twenty-six which served from September 1961 to March 1969.

Beauty and the beast – Miss Dorothy Trollope, twenty-one, taking part in a company's centenary celebrations and in Edwardian finery, poses in front of a Bristol Bloodhound, part of the 1959 ground exhibit. Propelled by two Bristol Siddeley Thor ramjets and launched by four Gosling rocket boosters, the Bloodhound was a Mach 2 missile and served with the RAF from 1958 to 1991. No further details are available on Miss Trollope!

Designed to succeed the Viscount, the Vickers Vanguard was powered by four Rolls-Royce Tyne turboprops of 4,985 or 5,545 shp, depending on the customer. BEA bought twenty with the smaller engine and TCA (who in 1964 became Canadian Pacific) twenty-three of the more powerful version. Capacity varied from 126 to 139 passengers but although it gave good service turboprops were being replaced by jets and there were no more orders. G-APEB at the 1959 show was BEA's second; it was broken up at Heathrow in June 1973. The last Vanguards in service were cargo versions, with Hunting Air Cargo, and were due to retire in 1996.

Handley Page's Dart Herald demonstrator G-AODF carried out demonstration tours of forty-four different countries in 1959 wearing BEA colours and with two 330 gallon underwing tanks. Here it rests in Spain alongside a CASA 2-111 (licence-built Heinkel He 111) before returning home to take part in the 1959 show. Later re-registered G-ARTC, it was broken up in 1962. Including two prototypes, fifty Heralds were built and served in many countries powered by two 1,910 shp Rolls-Royce Dart turboprops.

A general view of the 1960 park. In the foreground is de Havilland Sea Vixen FAW.1 XJ578 surrounded by a variety of weapons. Hawker Hunter FR.10 XG168 with underwing tanks and nose cameras is joined by the Hunter T.66A G-APUX, used as a demonstrator at a number of shows. At centre stage are Folland Gnat T.1s XM691 and '693.

Waiting to leap into the air in 1960 from the 'piano keys' is Lancashire Prospector 2 G-ARDG, a re-engined version of Edgar Percival's E.P.9 with a 375 hp Armstrong Siddeley Cheetah. Forty E.P.9s were built before the design was sold to Lancashire Aircraft Co who built seven Prospectors, but only one Cheetah-powered, the others having a 295 hp Lycoming. G-ARDG is one of three held by the Museum of Army Flying at Middle Wallop who intend to produce one flyer and one static aircraft from the components.

Avro Lincoln G-APRJ used by Napier for icing research had received B Conditions marks G-29-1 by 1960 and was shown again. Featuring a modified Lancaster nose, it tested flying surfaces mounted vertically on the fuselage and sprayed from an icing rig – the ladder-type apparatus visible. The Battle of Britain Memorial Flight's Lancaster PA474 had been used previously for the same work. The remains of G-29-1 were behind a hangar at North Weald in late 1995.

Armstrong Whitworth showed a pair of Argosy freighters at the 1959 and 1960 shows; G-APRL, the second prototype was at the latter, and was later fitted as seen here with the 'beaver' type doors installed on RAF Argosys. Powerplants were Rolls-Royce Dart turboprops of 2,020 to 2,470 ehp. Total production amounted to seventy-three, of which fifty-six were for the RAF. The seventeen civil aircraft served with BEA, several US cargo airlines and others.

Four
Into the Seventies
1961-1972

This period was marked mainly by developed versions of existing types with a scattering of new ones. Aircraft were becoming more complex and the gestation period was extending. One of the most important developments was the entry into service of the Hawker Siddeley Harrier in 1969, the world's first vertical take-off and landing fighter. It is still the only one in squadron service since Russia's Yak did not get this far, while the US AV-8B is the ultimate Harrier development.

The Fokker Friendship, first shown in 1966, proved highly successful and sold throughout the world; it exemplified the increasing showing of foreign aircraft with major British equipment which began that year and continued up to 1972 when any European aircraft could be shown – the Friendship's British equipment included the splendid Rolls-Royce Dart turboprop which was a real success story.

From 1974, the show went fully international but that is outside our parameters. Suffice to say that between 1966 and 1972, twenty-six different basic types of foreign aircraft and six representing international programmes were shown, and a lot of British equipment was included in these.

It was to be 1978 before a Dakota was to be seen at an SBAC show – and that was the very non-standard Specialised Aircraft Tri-Turbo Three with three Pratt & Whitney PT6 turboprops – and that is way beyond our scope here!

The 1961 static park with some familiar sights – the Napier Lincoln was again prominent. At the far end can be seen a production Handley Page Victor B.2 XL164, Herald G-ARTC (the former G-AODF) in Maritime Central Airways colours, Avro 748 G-ARMV and de Havilland Comet 4c G-AROV for Middle East Airlines (it actually went to Argentina as LV-PTS). The small triangle between them is the Handley Page H.P. 115 (see page 94).

Probably the oddest shape in 1961 was the Handley Page H.P. 115 XP841. Built to research flight characteristics of the narrow delta wing, it was powered by a 1,900 lb thrust Bristol Siddeley Viper turbojet giving useful low-speed handling experience for the Concorde project. It is preserved with a Concorde and other research aircraft at the Fleet Air Arm Museum, Yeovilton.

This view of the 1961 show gives an excellent impression of the airfield and runway, with the exhibition hall, chalets and car parks. Above the chalets and near the group of trees is the Empire Test Pilots' School hangar. After taking part in the flying display, aircraft are parked to the right of the runway, not visible here, being returned to the static area after the flying is finished or early the following morning.

Saunders-Roe Skeeters had been appearing at SBAC shows since 1952; by 1960 it had become the Westland Skeeter and XM563 was shown in 1960 and 1961 with a 425 shp Blackburn Turmo gas turbine in place of the 215 hp D.H. Gipsy Major piston engine in production Mk 12s. After trials, XM563 reverted to standard, joining No 652 Squadron, Army Air Corps in 1963.

Beagle made their first appearance in 1961, and the Auster ancestry was clear in the four-seat Airedale. With a 180 hp Lycoming engine, G-ARNP, the third production example, remained firmly in the static, while G-ARKE with a 175 hp Rolls-Royce Continental, was allowed to fly. Heavier and slower than contemporary Cessnas, the Airedale did not sell well and only forty-three were built. G-ARNP is one of the few survivors.

A pair of de Havilland Sea Vixen FAW.1s, XN694 and XJ571 from No 899 Squadron at Yeovilton demonstrated a flight refuelling hook up in 1962. The squadron was mainly shore-based but detachments were embarked on HMS *Centaur* and HMS *Hermes*. Both aircraft were later converted to FAW.2s, XJ571 becoming instructional airframe 8140M.

A corner of the 1962 static park. In the foreground, the third de Havilland Trident 1 G-ARPC for BEA (it was joined in the flying programme by 'RPA and 'RPB), the first D.H. 125 G-ARYA, Handley Page Herald CF-MCK for Maritime Central Airways and the prototype Vickers VC10 G-ARTA. On the right, behind Hawker Hunter T.66A G-APUX, is the Hawker P.1127 XP972.

Illustrating an export sale in 1962 was Avro 748 C-91 2500, the first of six for the Brazilian Air Force. More than 370 were built, with Rolls-Royce Dart turboprops, power ranging from 1,740 to 2,105 shp depending on variant. 748s served throughout the world and were second only to the Viscount in British airliners sold. Eighty-nine were built under licence in India.

Wg Cdr Ken Wallis built a number of autogyros and in 1962 demonstrated XR942, one of five built for Army evaluation, under the title Beagle-Wallis WA.116. This model had a 72 hp Wallis-McCulloch engine. Restored in 1966 as G-ARZA, its last known location was Deiniolen, Carmarthen in 1968, but at least eleven others are stored at Reymerston Hall, Norfolk.

Another part of the 1962 static shows Westland Whirlwind HAR.2 XK991, Whirlwind 3 G-APDY, Folland Gnat T.1 XM698, Hawker P.1127 XP972 and Hunter T.66A G-APUX which features in a number of views. There seems to be some indiscriminate car parking in the foreground!

Touching down on the 'piano keys' in 1962 is the prototype Vickers VC10 G-ARTA, with photographers taking their life in their hands! Early VC10s had four 21,000 lb Rolls-Royce Conway engines. Fifty-four were built comprising thirty-three standard and twenty-one Super VC10s, the latter having 22,500 lb Conways. Both versions served mainly with BOAC, but other customers included British United, Ghana and East African Airways. The RAF had fourteen and a number of these are still flying after conversion to air-to-air refuelling configuration. G-ARTA was damaged beyond repair at Gatwick on 28 January 1972.

One end of the 1962 static park was dominated by Avro Vulcan B.2 XL381 with a Blue Steel missile beneath the belly. Next to it, also in 'anti-radiation' white finish is Blackburn Buccaneer S.1 XN929, while opposite is Bristol Britannia C.1 XL640 *Antares*, one of twenty-three supplied to the RAF.

Instead of the usual hovering view, here is the third prototype Hawker P.1127 XP972 in the 1962 static. It had a 10,500 lb Bristol Pegasus vectored-thrust turbofan at this time but with development engines installed thrust rose to 13,500 lb. XP972 was destroyed on 30 October that year after an in-flight fire necessitated a forced landing on the disused Tangmere airfield.

The Bristol 188 was built of stainless steel for research into heating effect on aircraft structures at Mach 2 for the Concorde programme. Powered by two 14,000 lb de Havilland Gyron Junior turbojets, two were built, XF923 and '926. The first appeared at the 1962 show; both were, on completion of their test programmes, sent to Shoeburyness as gunnery targets but the second was recovered, became 8368M and is preserved as XF926 at the Cosford Aerospace Museum.

With only ten hours flying time on the clock, G-ARYA, the first de Havilland D.H.125 executive jet appeared at the 1962 show. It had two 3,000 lb Bristol Siddeley Viper turbojets, was the first of more than 900 built to date in various versions and is still in production; 125s serve throughout the world with civil and military customers. G-ARYA was withdrawn from use at Chester in October 1965.

Three Short Belfasts were shown in 1964, two of which, XR362 and '363, appeared only in the flying programme. Ten were built for the RAF, serving from 1966 to 1976, phased out due to defence cuts. Six were bought by cargo operator HeavyLift, three were scrapped by Rolls-Royce who acquired their 5,730 shp Tyne turboprops and one, XR371, is preserved at the Cosford Aerospace Museum. At least two were still current with HeavyLift in early 1996.

Part of the sixty-aircraft assault on the airfield in 1964 were twenty-four Westland Wessex, twelve HAS.5s from No 849 Squadron, Culdrose providing the naval element while from the RAF came twelve HC.2s from No 18 Squadron, Odiham. Five of the latter are shown, XR499/A, XR506/H, XR518/L, XR516/E and XR510/O. Other Wessex in the distance include four with underslung Land Rovers.

The handsome Beagle B.206, shown in prototype form in 1961 and 1962, was present in 1964 with the first Series 1, G-ASMK, with 310 hp Rolls-Royce Continental engines. More than eighty were built including twenty for the RAF as the Basset, while fourteen were exported. G-ASMK was withdrawn from use in 1966 following damage in storage.

Newest and most successful aircraft shown in 1964 were the two prototype Britten-Norman Islanders, G-ATCT and 'TWU, the latter in Loganair titles. Production aircraft had 260 hp Lycoming engines; the type is still being built more than thirty years later with more than 1,200 sold, including the three-engined Trislander development. G-ATCT was lost in a crash in Holland during November 1966 and 'TWU was later converted into the prototype Trislander.

A novel way of showing Westland Wasp HAS.1 XT414 in 1964. The first of a second batch of thirty, it was used as a trials aircraft, including Mk 44 torpedo dropping. Powered by a 1,050 shp Bristol Siddeley Nimbus turboshaft, more than 130 Wasps were built for the Royal Navy, the navies of Brazil, The Netherlands and Indonesia, and the New Zealand and South African Air Forces.

The international Transall programme built the C.160 transport and the prototype appeared in 1966. Powered by 6,100 shp Rolls-Royce Tyne turboprops, it went into production in France and Germany and 175 were built, fifty-three for France, ninety-seven for Germany, sixteen for Turkey and nine for South Africa. A further twenty-nine Srs 2 aircraft were built for France.

A Commonwealth newcomer in 1966 which would subsequently appear at many SBAC shows was the de Havilland Canada Twin Otter, Powered by 579 ehp Pratt & Whitney PT6A turboprops, CF-UXE in the colours of Trans-Australia Airlines was a Series 100, the eighth production aircraft. It did not go to TAA, but to Air Caledonia as F-OCFJ.

The English Electric Lightning appeared in various forms from 1955 when the P.1 prototype was shown. By 1966 it had become the BAC Lightning and had reached the ultimate RAF mark, the F.6. An RAF aircraft, XR770, appeared in Royal Saudi Air Force colours in which service it was designated F.53. The two 12,690 lb Rolls-Royce Avon turbojets were mounted one above the other. The RAF received 278 Lightnings which served from December 1959 to 1988, although Phantoms had replaced most by the mid-1970s.

Farthest flung display aircraft in 1968 was the Japanese NAMC YS-11A airliner, permitted by virtue of its 3,060 ehp Rolls-Royce Dart turboprops. JA-8714 featured a large cargo door in the forward fuselage, being a 'combi' with accommodation for cargo and forty-six passengers, the all-passenger version could carry sixty. Total production reached 182.

Current production version of the D.H. Trident – by 1968 the Hawker Siddeley Trident – was the Series Two powered by three 11,960 lb Rolls-Royce Spey turbofans. G-AVFI, landing at Farnborough, was a 2E, one of fifteen built for BEA, the world's first airliners to have full all-weather automatic landing systems. Two 2Es were built for Cyprus Airways and thirty-three for CAAC, China. G-AVFI was broken up in May 1982.

Yugoslavia was another newcomer in 1968 with a pair of Soko jets, the two-seat Galeb 23268 illustrated and the basically similar single-seat ground attack Jastreb 24031. Both were powered by a single Rolls-Royce Viper turbojet of 3,395 and 3,000 lb respectively. Both types were supplied to the air forces of Yugoslavia and Zambia.

Demonstrating its aerobatic capabilities is the Beagle Pup 150 G-AVLN, the fourth production aircraft and one of five exhibited in 1968, Powered by a 150 hp Lycoming engine, it is believed to still exist in a store at Manston. Total Pup production reached 152 of which sixty were exported before Beagle went into receivership. Pups were also available with a 100 hp Rolls-Royce Continental or 160 hp Lycoming engine.

Export versions for Saudi Arabia of the BAC Lightning F.53 and Strikemaster 80 were shown side by side in 1968. The Strikemaster, developed from the Jet Provost, was powered by a 3,410 lb Rolls-Royce Viper turbojet and was very successful in export markets, 146 being ordered. Deliveries had been completed by 1978.

In 1968 production models of the Hawker Siddeley Harrier appeared for the first time at Farnborough and four aircraft flew – XV739, '740, '742 and '743 – three of these are shown. Harriers or Sea Harriers have been at most shows ever since. XV739 crashed in Cyprus in September 1973; '742 was used for demonstration in US Marine Corps colours and was registered G-VSTO for a time; '743 crashed at Dunsfold in January 1969.

Short revealed the latest version of the Skyvan at the 1970 show; G-ASZJ was the Skyliner in British Air Services colours. When the Skyvan first flew in January 1963 it had Continental piston engines but early production models had Turboméca Astazou turboprops; from the tenth aircraft onwards 715 shp Garrett-AiResearch turboprops were fitted. More than 250 Skyvans were built for civil and military users; G-ASZJ is still currently registered.

The BAC One-Eleven 475 was designed for short runways and unsealed strips. First shown at Farnborough in 1964, the type had developed through several series and the 475 was present in 1970. More than 250 were built for sale to many countries and a number are still in service. G-ASYD in Series 475 form had 12,550 lb Rolls-Royce Spey engines; it is preserved at the Brooklands Museum.

An ingenious modification to the second prototype Britten-Norman Islander G-ATWU was the lengthening of the fuselage and addition of a third engine above the tail to produce the eighteen-seat Trislander, first flown in 11 September 1970 and flown to the show that afternoon. A number were sold, mostly abroad, but ten were operated by Channel Islands airline Aurigny. Trislanders have 260 hp Lycoming engines; G-ATWU was withdrawn from use at Bembridge in November 1970.

Prince Charles tries the Campbell Cricket G-AXVK for size in 1970. This example was powered by a modified 1600 cc Volkswagen engine and appeared in the flying display. It is believed to be still in existence in Barnstaple.

The Cierva Rotorcraft Mk III Grasshopper G-AWRP was powered by two 135 hp Rolls-Royce Continental engines driving co-axial contra-rotating two-blade rotors. It had been under development at Redhill for several years and made a brief appearance at Farnborough in 1970. This view, before the registration was applied, was chosen to show the rotor blade/head configuration. The Grasshopper is preserved at the International Helicopter Museum, Weston-super-Mare.

Shown in 1970 by virtue of its licence-built 15,000 lb Rolls-Royce Spey engine (Allison TF-41), the A-7E Corsair 156888 carrier-based attack aircraft was one of two from the USS *Kittyhawk*, the first American combat aircraft to appear at a SBAC show. Notable in this view are the extended arrester hook and flight refuelling probe, also the twin nose wheels.

The jet reigns supreme in this corner of the 1970 static park. In the foreground, BAC Jet Provost T.5 XW318, Strikemaster 84 315/G-AYHT, one of two shown for the Singapore Air Defence Command, Lightning F.2A XN733 and SEPECAT Jaguar M.05 in French markings. Across the way are the two-seat Hawker Siddeley Harrier XW175 plus single-seater XV742 in US Marine Corps colours, HS.125-400 G-AXYJ, Buccaneer S.2A XV350 and HS.748-2 G-AVXI.

It may be the world's most photographed aircraft but we could not omit Concorde. Here, the British prototype G-BSST, appearing only in the 1970 flying programme, makes its approach over the RAE police gate. G-BSST is preserved at the Fleet Air Arm Museum, Yeovilton.

111

India was represented for the first time in 1972 by the indigenous Hindustan Kiran trainer U-703, powered by a 2,500 lb Rolls-Royce Viper turbojet. Around 190 Kirans were built for the Indian Air Force, some of the later models being ground attack versions.

Also from India were a pair of Hindustan Gnats, E1069 and '1070. India received two ex-British Gnats and twenty-three UK-built aircraft plus twenty kits of components for assembly by Hindustan Aircraft. HAL then undertook licence manufacture and built 195, the last two of which became prototypes of the HAL Ajeet. The Gnats were powered by a 4,705 lb Rolls-Royce Orpheus.

Making its debut in 1972 was the mighty SAAB Viggen AJ37, the second prototype, 37002, being shown. Production aircraft had a 16,200 lb Volvo RM8B turbofan and 329 of varying marks were built for the Swedish Air Force. A large aircraft, the Viggen was always an impressive beast to watch at displays.

Australia was represented in 1972 by the Government Aircraft Factory Nomad N22 VH-SUR, shown off its STOL characteristics. Powered by 400 shp Allison turboprops, 170 Nomads were built in military and civil versions. Deliveries of the latter started in 1975 to the Royal Flying Doctor Service; VH-SUR was the second prototype

The first production Fokker F.28-2000 made its public debut at Farnborough in 1972 alongside a F.27-400M. The F.28, a seventy-nine seater, had two 9,900 lb Rolls-Royce Spey turbojets; PH-ZAX was a temporary registration and the aircraft was delivered to Nigeria Airways. Production of the F.28 ended in 1986 when 241 had been ordered by fifty-seven customers in thirty-seven countries; it was succeeded by the Fokker 100.

Largest aircraft to be shown at Farnborough under the British engine or equipment rule before the show went fully international in 1974 was the Lockheed TriStar with three 42,000 Rolls-Royce RB211 engines. Exhibited was N305EA, the fifth of five on order by Eastern Airlines but painted in a pseudo BEA scheme. There were long queues to see the interior; BEA and BOAC were merged in the early 1970s as British Airways who received twenty-one TriStars.

Five
Engine Test Beds

When aero-engines of a new or modified design need to be tested in their natural environment it has been the practice to install them in a proven airframe, either in place of the standard powerplant or as an 'add-on' to existing engines.

A number of these test-beds have been displayed at SBAC shows; the earliest illustrated in this section are an Airspeed Courier with a Napier Rapier engine and Hawker Hart used to test the Bristol Pegasus, both pre-war examples.

Post-war there was a profusion of engines attached to various types; Avro Lancasters and Lancastrians were easy to come by from surplus stocks and were ideally suited to the task. They were succeeded by Avro Lincolns which were also plentiful and had their experimental engines under the wings, in the bomb bays or in the nose. Airliners were not exempt from this task as may be seen by the Rolls-Royce Nene-powered Avro Tudor and Vickers Viking, the Tay Viscount and the Airspeed Ambassador which tested several turboprops. Even the trusty Dakota was fitted with Armstrong Siddeley Mamba and Rolls-Royce Dart turboprops but since they were not shown at any SBAC event they are not illustrated here.

Gloster Meteors and English Electric Canberras were also favourites for hanging things on, even the humble de Havilland Chipmunk tested two turboprops but only one is within our timescale.

Today there are few types used for engine trials; the heyday of this has passed but Boeing 707s and 747s may be seen with one engine larger than the others.

1934 and the Airspeed Courier was the first British production aircraft to be fitted with a retractable undercarriage, but examples were also built with fixed gear. Shown was G-ACNZ, bought by D. Napier & Sons as a test-bed for their 325 hp Rapier IV air-cooled engine. It later reverted to the standard 240 hp Armstrong Siddeley Lynx radial, was impressed in March 1940 as X9346, serving with No 3 Ferry Pilots Pool and Airspeed until SOC on 12 April 1944.

Several Hawker Harts were used as engine test-beds; K3020 was shown in 1937 with a Bristol Pegasus in a long-chord cowling. It later carried out the certification programme of the Bristol Mercury installation for the Bristol Blenheim and tested Bristol Perseus and Taurus components for the prototype Beaufort. It became instructional airframe 1169M in February 1939.

Avro Lancaster III TW911 with 3,670 ehp Armstrong Siddeley Python turboprops in place of the outboard Rolls-Royce Merlins landing at Farnborough in 1949. The Pythons drove contra-rotating propellers; at least fourteen Lancasters served as engine test-beds. TW911 was SOC on 17 January 1953.

Ten Avro Lincolns were used to test eight different types of engine; RF530 had a 1,500 ehp Napier Naiad turboprop in the nose at the 1948 show. The Lincoln subsequently passed to Rolls-Royce in February 1957 as G-37-1 to test the Tyne (see below).

Rolls-Royce received Lincoln RF530 from Napier and installed the prototype 4,500 shp Tyne turboprop in the nose as part of the Vickers Vanguard development programme. It flew at the 1956 show on the power of the Tyne alone, but here the Tyne is resting. Note strengthening between the bomb bay and tail. G-37-1 was scrapped in January 1966.

With Bristol Brabazon G-AGPW waiting to take-off, Lincoln SX972 with 3,200 ehp Bristol Proteus turboprops in the outer nacelles comes in to land at the 1950 or '51 show – both types were present on both occasions. The Lincoln was SOC on 21 July 1953.

Lincoln SX973 was allocated to Napier to test the Nomad turboprop in the nose. The Nomad developed 3,000 shp and was shown in the Lincoln at the 1951 show. After completion of the tests, SX973 was SOC on 13 May 1953.

The Handley Page (ex Miles) Marathon G-AHXU was fitted experimentally with two 1,010 shp Armstrong Siddeley Mamba turboprops and appeared in 1950. By the following year it had become VX231 and by 1955 had been converted to test Alvis Leonides piston engines under the designation H.P.R.5. Development of this engine was discontinued in 1958 and VX231 was scrapped at Bitteswell in October 1959.

The second prototype Vickers Varsity was converted to test the 3,000 ehp Napier Eland turboprop which first ran in August 1952. Flight trials began in summer 1954 and the programme also included Eland installations in an Airspeed Ambassador and Convair 340. The Varsity VX835 appeared at the 1954 show; a later development of the Eland gave 4,000 ehp.

In 1956 the Bristol Britannia prototype G-ALBO flies past with its two inner 3,780 ehp Bristol Proteus turboprops stopped. The other two engines were a 3,900 ehp Proteus and, with a white cowling, a 5,500 ehp Bristol Orion. G-ALBO left its Bristol, Filton birthplace on its last flight on 30 November 1960 to RAF St Athan where it became instructional airframe 7708M.

The third Airspeed Ambassador, the production prototype G-ALFR, was loaned to Napier in 1954 for development flying of the 3,000 ehp Eland turboprop, a programme shared by the Eland Varsity and Convair 340 (see page 119). On completion of the tests, G-ALFR was returned to standard configuration and sold to Dan-Air who operated it from January 1964 to autumn 1967 before withdrawing it from use at Lasham.

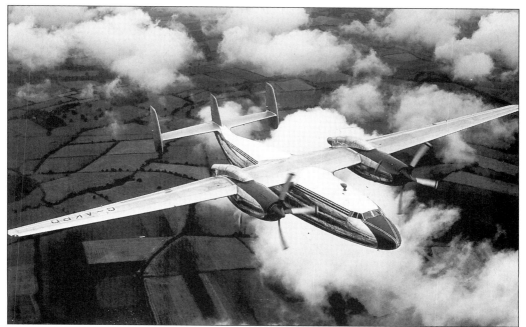

At the 1954 show, the second prototype Ambassador, G-AKRD, displayed the 3,780 ehp Bristol Proteus turboprops which it was testing. In 1958 it passed to Rolls-Royce for tests with their Tyne and Dart engines for over ten years as G-37-3. After restoration to standard as G-AKRD, it was eventually broken up at Hucknall in October 1969.

Two prototypes of the Short Sperrin were built as an insurance against any failure in the V-bomber programme.VX158 had four 6,500 lb Rolls-Royce Avons, while VX161 had 7,500 lb Avons. Both performed useful research tasks; VX158 was fitted with a 15,000 de Havilland Gyron turbojet in place of the port lower Avon in 1955 and the following year a second was installed as seen here. Both aircraft were scrapped in 1957 and 1958.

An early production English Electric Canberra B.2, WD952 was used as a test-bed for the 8,000 lb Bristol Olympus turbojet intended for the Avro Vulcan B.1 and developed from 11,000 to 13,500 lb in that mark. On 4 May 1953 WD952 established a new height record of 63,668 ft and with more powerful engines this was pushed to 65,889 ft on 29 August 1955. Both records were listed on the nose when it appeared in the 1955 show.

Another Canberra B.2, WK163 powered by two 6,500 lb Rolls-Royce Avons and with a Napier Double Scorpion rocket engine at the rear of the bomb bay, broke WD952's record on 28 August 1957, reaching 70,310 ft. WK163 is preserved at Bruntingthorpe; these two Canberras represent a number used for engine testing.

Several Avro Lancastrians were among the types used to test jet engines – Rolls-Royce Avons and Nenes, and de Havilland Ghosts. VM703 was one of two flown with 5,500 lb Ghosts in place of the outer Rolls-Royce Merlins. Appearing at the 1947 show at Radlett, it is here flying on Ghost power alone. It was SOC on 23 June 1950.

The 107th Vickers Viking airframe was completed for the Ministry of Supply with two 5,000 lb Rolls-Royce Nene turbojets and other modifications to become Britain's first jet transport. Registered G-AJPH, it later wore military marks VX856 and flew from London Airport to Paris/Villacoublay in 34 minutes on 25 July 1948. It was later converted to standard configuration with 1,690 hp Bristol Hercules engines and a cargo door, sold to Eagle Aviation and used for several years before being scrapped at Blackbushe in September 1962.

The second jet-powered airliner shown in 1948 was the Avro Tudor 8, VX195. Converted from the second prototype Tudor 1 via a brief period as a Tudor 4, it had four 5,000 lb Rolls-Royce Nenes in paired nacelles. After various tests at Boscombe Down it was broken up in 1951 at Farnborough.

The second prototype Vickers Viscount was completed as a test-bed for the Rolls-Royce Tay turbojet, becoming VX217. It appeared at the 1950 show and was later used by Boulton Paul for powered-control trials, including those for the Vickers Valiant.

Developed from the Avro Tudor but with a tricycle undercarriage, the six Ashtons built were used for research and engine testing. The second, WB491, appeared at the 1955 show with a 17,500 lb Rolls-Royce Conway engine which was intended for BOAC Boeing 707s. The Ashton was later used to test the nacelle of an Armstrong Siddeley Sapphire with icing rig.

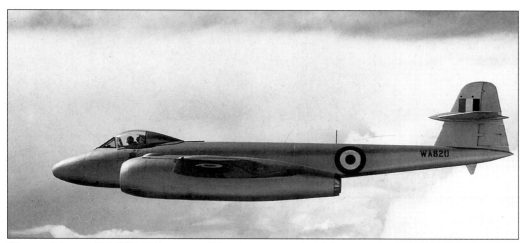

Gloster Meteor F.8 WA820 was used by Armstrong Siddeley to test their Sapphire engines, rated at around 7,500 lb, and appeared in this form at the 1950 and 1951 shows – the much larger nacelles and tail bumper are noticeable. It established four time to height records on 31 August 1951, including 3 minutes 9.5 seconds to 12,000 m. WA820 eventually passed to the Central Fighter Establishment, becoming instructional airframe 7141M on 31 March 1954.

Another Meteor used for engine testing was F.8 WA982 which had a pair of 1,810 lb Rolls-Royce Soar turbojets mounted on the wing tips. They weighed only 267 lb each and the aircraft appeared at the 1954 show. It was eventually converted to a Mk U.16 target drone.

Gloster Javelin FAW.1 XA552, the ninth production aircraft, was modified to test two 14,000 lb de Havilland Gyron Junior engines for the Bristol 188 (see page 100). It was painted royal blue with white trim and is shown landing in 1951.

Avro Vulcan XA903 replaced XA894 as an engine test-bed at Filton in January 1964. It accumulated over 400 hours of test flying in the Concorde programme with a Bristol Olympus 593 in a Concorde pod beneath the fuselage in which form it appeared at Farnborough in 1966. In 1973 it tested the RB199 engine intended for the Panavia Tornado in 285 hours flying before being retired in March 1979.

Vulcan XA894 tested the Bristol Olympus for the BAC TSR.2. Slung beneath the centre section, it had a bifurcated intake and carried out about eighty hours of tests before being burnt out on the ground at Filton on 3 December 1962. It had appeared at Farnborough that year.

RAF Vickers VC10 XR809 was delivered to Rolls-Royce in 1969 and its two Rolls-Royce Conway turbofans on the left side were replaced by a 42,000 lb RB211 for a 1,000 hour test of typical Lockheed TriStar airliner operations before the TriStar's first flight in November 1970. The VC10 was displayed at the 1970 show as G-AXLR; it returned to standard and rejoined the RAF in May 1973.

We end on a small note – de Havilland Chipmunk G-ATTS was a 1966 exhibit fitted with a 100 hp Rover Wolston turboprop by Hants and Sussex Aviation. Ex 7650M and WP895, it was a one-off conversion and was sold in October 1969 to the USA as N2247.